THE
GOOD
LUCK
BOOK

THE
GOOD LUCK BOOK

AN A-TO-Z GUIDE
TO CHARMS AND SYMBOLS
BY BILL HARRIS

Ottenheimer
PUBLISHERS, INC

INTRODUCTION

One day, millions of years ago, one of our ancestors narrowly escaped the clutches of a saber-toothed tiger. Not long afterward, lightning struck nearby but no one in the prehistoric family was hit. Then a tree fell across the entrance to their cave minutes after one of the children had gone inside. That night they began to ponder what all these things meant. Something strange was going on out there. What it was, was luck!

Being human, it was just as important for our ancestors to figure out *why* it was. After all, this luck thing had possibilities. It needed to be encouraged. What did all these events have in common? Was it something someone in the family was wearing? Was it something they were carrying? Eventually the family conference may have narrowed it down to a single thing. Maybe it was the animal skin the hunter wore. Possibly it was the axe head or piece of stone one of them carried. Whatever it was, it became the world's first lucky charm. And charms in all shapes and sizes have been with us ever since.

Some charms can make you healthy, some can make you happy, others can help you find a lover (or keep one). Some lucky charms have the power to make you rich or beautiful, or both. They can confound your enemies, protect your family, make your house secure. In just about every case, a lucky charm works its own special magic by summoning good spirits to counteract the forces of evil that are all around us.

In our enlightened age, some people say there is no such thing as luck. But they might cross their fingers when they say it. If luck doesn't exist, how do they explain why millions buy lottery tickets in spite of crushing odds against winning the jackpot? Somebody eventually wins. And that somebody has luck on their side.

If there is such a thing as good luck, there is also bad luck, which should be avoided. Some people will walk under a ladder, but most can't do it without a fleeting thought that it might be a foolish thing to do. Would a sensible bride walk down the aisle without "something old, something new, something borrowed, something blue"? And why do Americans spend more than $130 million a year on good luck charms? Does it mean that we are a superstitious people? Probably. But wearing a charm for luck can't hurt. And for all anyone knows, it might help.

Luck is probably the most universal belief in the entire human race. Everyone has experienced it at one time or another. It might have been a narrow escape from death or injury, a chance meeting that led to a turning point in your life, finding something valuable others had overlooked and, yes, winning the lottery.

In most cultures such things are seen as something magical, but the ancient Romans had a slightly more active view. Among their words of wisdom: *Audaces fortuna juvat*, "Luck does not favor hesitation." It is all well and good to carry a rabbit's foot on your key chain or a four-leaf clover in your wallet, but when all is said and done, the best way to attract good luck is to go for it.

You can help luck along. All you need is the appropriate good luck charm. Many are described on the following pages. Most have been used for thousands of years, and belief in them still runs strong all over the world. Humbug? Who's to say? After all, challenging these time-honored beliefs just might result in a run of bad luck.

ABRACADABRA

Usually associated with magicians who pull rabbits from hats, the word *abracadabra* has much more power than you may think.

It is what is known as a sigil, a mystical word. It can become a lucky talisman if it is written on a piece of parchment and worn around the neck in a pouch made of clean leather. To work its special magic, usually to heal an illness, it should be worn for nine days. Then the wearer should remove it and toss it over the left shoulder into a running stream.

Simply writing the word won't do the trick. It must be written by someone who is pure of heart, preferably after a period of fasting. The lines for writing it must be drawn on the rough side of the parchment, but the writing itself must be on the smooth side. The letters, which must not touch one another, are arranged to form an inverted triangle. The word is written in full on the top line and one letter is dropped for each line below it until only one letter is left. It should look something like this:

```
A B R A C A D A B R A
A B R A C A D A B R
A B R A C A D A B
A B R A C A D A
A B R A C A D
A B R A C A
A B R A C
A B R A
A B R
A B
A
```

The word is believed to have even stronger power written in Hebrew letters. One reason is that it is expressed in nine letters when the Hebrew alphabet is used. Nine is a multiple of three and because of that it is usually regarded as a powerful number. When the word is arranged as a triangle, aleph, the alphabet's first letter, a symbol of beginnings and good intentions, is repeated nine times from the bottom to the top left, greatly enhancing the magic of the word.

The origin of the word itself is lost in the mists of time. One theory is that it was the name given to some ancient demon. People once believed that knowing the name of a supernatural being gave them power over it. The children's story of Rumpelstiltskin is a good example of such a belief. Once his name was guessed, his power left him and he vanished in a rage of defeat.

The word *abracadabra* was used by ancient cultures as far back as the Persians as an incantation to reduce fevers. The patient began by reciting the whole word, then repeated it over and over, dropping a letter each time it was pronounced. As each letter was lost, a little bit of the sickness was believed to be lost with it, until the final A was spoken and it would vanish completely. Although the exercise was also thought useful in dealing with such things as toothaches, there is no record that it can cure hiccups. But it's worth a try.

Abraxas Stone

Not often found these days, except in museums, abraxas stones were among the most common talismans worn in the Middle Ages. They take their name from the word *abraxas* which was always engraved on them in Greek letters. It represents the number 365, which, apart from the fact it is the number of days in the year, refers to the number of spirits the ancients believed emanated from the Supreme Deity. The word was used along with carved figures, the most common of which was a creature with the head of a rooster (for watchfulness), and the body of a man holding a whip of power and a shield of wisdom. The creature's legs were a pair of serpents, which symbolized inner light and understanding. The perceived power of the stones, to repel all evil and attract good fortune, originated among the Gnostics, a powerful sect that emerged in the early Christian era. Their beliefs incorporated the teachings of the Jewish Talmud, the religions of ancient Egypt, Buddhism and Christianity.

Acorn

Long before they began exploring the world in their long-boats, the Vikings associated oak trees with Thor, the god who created thunder and lightning with his great anvil and hammer. Because the tree attracted lightning, they believed it was sacred to Thor. But they also believed that the acorn, the fruit of the tree, was always spared the god's wrath, and so they began putting acorns on window sills to protect their houses.

When the Vikings began roaming, one of their first stops was the British Isles, and they may have been quite surprised to discover that the mysterious Druids there also put great store in the luck of the acorn. But theirs was a different kind of luck. The Druids worshiped the oak as a symbol of strength and long life and wore acorns around their necks as amulets to bring that strength to themselves.

In modern times, acorns, either real or wooden imitations, are often placed near windows or hung from window-shade pulls to bring luck to the house.

Adornment

If you have ever wondered why we wear jewelry in the exact places we do, stop thinking that it is because the places chosen are the most accessible or make the most sense. In the past, it was common belief that evil spirits and demons could only enter the body through the main orifices. It would then make sense to place jewels or metals near those areas to prevent demonic possession.

Therefore, earrings dangling near two openings in the body protected the ears from allowing a devil passage into the body. In India, noserings were used for the same reason, as were tattoos and designs around the mouth and eyes.

The tradition of fingernail and toenail painting originated because of a need to protect oneself from demonic entrance. Nails of the toes and fingers were painted so that the demons could not penetrate the skin in these vulnerable areas and gain access to the body.

The most protective article of jewelry by far was the ring. Since it is in the form of a continuous circle, it symbolized eternity and unity. It was also believed that certain stones and metals gain power over time and that they are affected by the good or bad luck of their wearers.

ADRIAN, SAINT

A native of Africa, Adrian became a monk in Italy in the seventh century. After refusing an offer to become the Archbishop of Canterbury, he went to England to found a boy's school there. After his death, many miracles were attributed to him, particularly influencing the lives of his students. Today he is said to bring luck to boys who get in trouble with their teachers.

AGATE

The ancient Romans believed that wearing an agate in a ring would bring special favor from the gods. Over time, the stone became a lucky charm for people who work the soil. It has the power, some say, to make crops thrive in places other-wise barren, and the multicolored stone is more effective than a green thumb for making your garden grow. In the Far East, agates are said to promote eloquence. They also have the power to bring good fortune in the form of an inheritance. And if you aren't lucky enough to have rich, old relatives, some people say an agate can lead you to hidden treasure. In Islam, an agate crushed to dust and drunk in apple juice is believed to have the power to cure insanity. In some cultures, the same recipe is an antidote to snakebite.

ALEXANDRITE

Alexandrite is a stone that has particularly strong powers in the areas of luck and love. Even though this stone is rather difficult to find and expensive once located, it draws luck and good fortune to the bearer.

If you are looking for good luck in love or friendship, try wearing a pendant of alexandrite near your heart so that love and fortune will find you more easily.

ALMOND

There isn't a tree that grows that doesn't have some significance in the world of luck. Among them, the almond has the power to attract undying love. The tradition goes back to the Greek legend of Demophon and Phyllis. According to the tale, Demophon, a soldier, promised to marry Phyllis, a princess, but showed up for the ceremony several months late. By the time he arrived, the poor princess, thinking she was rejected, had hanged herself. But the gods were moved and turned Phyllis into an almond tree. When Demophon offered a sacrifice to the tree it blossomed on the spot, even though no other tree in sight had produced any flowers.

In many parts of the world, the almond is the first tree to bloom in the spring. But because its blossoms are often blighted by cold, the symbolism of the tree's fruit sometimes refers to the impetuousness of youth. Combined with undying affection, on the other hand, an almond as a lucky charm can bring the sweetness of young love with an assurance that it will last.

AMBER

The Greeks called this stone elektron, which gave us our word for electricity, and its power to give off sparks when rubbed gives us a clue why even prehistoric people may have considered amber a lucky charm. Amber beads have been found in ancient tombs from the steppes of Russia to the shores of the Mediterranean. And almost every culture has regarded amber as a bit of the sun with the power to bring good fortune to anyone who held it. Both the Chinese and the Muslims burn amber as incense as a protection against evil spirits. Worn as a necklace, it was believed to have medicinal qualities, effective against everything from deafness to indigestion to tooth loss.

AMETHYST

For persons born under the sign of Aquarius, amethyst rings or necklaces bring luck through self-discipline.

Because the stone is the color of wine, the ancient Greeks, as well as many cultures that followed them, believed that it could prevent drunkenness. They made goblets of amethyst so they could drink to their heart's content and still find their way home.

Amethysts are also believed to encourage moderation, and in the Middle Ages they were the stone of choice for bishop's rings. In the Middle Ages, rosaries made of amethyst were used in wartime and during plagues. It was believed that the stone had a calming effect, helpful at such times. Some modern psychiatrists hold to the belief, which dates back to early Egypt, that the purple color of the stone can bring a kind of peace.

AMULET

An amulet is almost any natural object that brings luck, such as a rabbit's foot, a four-leaf clover or a birthstone, used in a necklace, a bracelet or other form of jewelry. In general, it is intended as a protective device that wards off illness, evil or harm, and secures good fortune. Although in modern times the word is synonymous with talismans or charms, its original meaning referred to things that occur in nature rather than something man-made, such as horseshoes and lucky coins.

ANCHOR

Among the early Christians, the anchor was a symbol of hope and salvation. It is also an obvious lucky charm for sailors, who regard the anchor as a promise of safe return from their voyages.

ANGEL

As a symbol of the invisible forces between heaven and earth, an angel is the most perfect of protectors and bringers of good luck. The ancient Hebrews believed that there were seven archangels and that their names, written in red on parchment, became a lucky talisman. They also believed in the special protection of twelve more angels, known as the massolith, each of whom commanded thirty generals with thirty angelic legions. Each legion consisted of thirty leaders with thirty captains under them, each in turn with thirty angels to command. These angels, the Hebrews believed, were the guardians of the land of Israel. In our time, many believe that every one of us has our own personal guardian angel to guide us away from evil and into God's holy ways.

ANKH

The symbol of a cross topped with a loop comes to us from ancient Egypt where it was an indispensable lucky charm for the pharaohs, who regarded it as a symbol of eternal life.

APPLE

In the Islamic world, there is an old tradition that apples have the power to cure almost any ill. In the Western world we say that an apple a day keeps the doctor away. But apples can do much more than cure what ails you. In many parts of America, they can help you discover if you'll be lucky in love, especially at Halloween. One tradition says that if you twist the stem of an apple, assigning a letter of the alphabet to each turn, the stem will break off when you've reached the initial of some-one who loves you. Another says that if you peel an apple and toss the skin over your left shoulder, it will land in the form of the initial of your true love. Yet another belief holds that if a group of people each tosses an apple into a tub of water and everyone takes turns trying to pick one up with his or her teeth, the person whose apple you catch will be your partner in marriage.

Old Norse legends say that the gods secured eternal youth by eating apples. The Greeks also believed the fruit guaranteed long life. In fact, one of the only times time you'll ever hear anything negative about the apple is in the story of Adam and Eve, in which the first woman is tempted by one. Yet, the Bible never said it was an apple at all. That came much later. According to Genesis, Eve picked the fruit of an unidentified tree in the midst of the garden. The serpent implied it was the tree of knowledge and among ancient people interpreting the story, that could only mean one thing: an apple tree. Although apples have been regarded as symbols of temptation ever since, they are still believed to have the power to bring luck, long life, and knowledge.

Aquamarine

In the Middle Ages, aquamarine necklaces were frequently worn to prevent or to cure toothaches and sore throats. In our time, the stone's meaning has become something quite different. As a lucky charm given by a man to his wife on their wedding day, it provides insurance for a happy marriage. It also, they say, helps assure constancy among lovers.

Arch

For generations, the English have believed that walking under an arch formed by intertwining blackberry bushes will cure rheumatism, boils, blackheads and whooping cough. In Bulgaria, they say the arch should be made by the overhanging branches of a willow tree, and walking under one will cure just whooping cough. Arches formed by the branches of an ash tree are favored in both France and Germany as a way to make dry cows produce milk again. All that is necessary, they say, is to drive the cow under one.

Armand, Saint

A seventh-century Catholic missionary, Saint Armand is credited with establishing Christianity in northern France and Belgium. In those regions today, people who honor his memory will have good luck in their vineyards. He also brings luck to brewers of beer, and anyone associated with the production and sale of alcoholic beverages.

ARROWHEAD

The ancients carved arrowheads from flint, and over the centuries, long after their hunts were forgotten, other people found them and believed that these triangular bits of stone had been fashioned by the gods and must have supernatural powers. As lucky charms, these flints were believed to have special power to attract love and to repel the effects of the evil eye. The arrow itself has become a lucky charm for lovers when it pierces two hearts and binds them together.

ASH

In most of Europe, the ashes from consecrated palms burned on Easter are mixed with seeds to insure healthy crops. In India, ashes from sacred fires are kept in houses to ward off devils and evil spirits. The Native Americans of the Pacific Northwest prepared for battle by burning wasps and rubbing the resulting ashes on warriors' bodies to bring them luck.

AVENTURINE

If you enjoy games of chance and gambling, aventurine could help you to increase your mental powers and sharpen your mind. This stone has a strong power of luck associated with it, and is indispensable to those seeking success in money, peace, and health.

Wearing green aventurine is said to enhance eyesight and perception, stimulate creativity and increase intelligence.

Aventurine is often used by those who enjoy games of chance and is prevalent as a gambler's pendant. This stone is also said to aid in business transactions since it has the power to attract money.

If you are having difficulty with a long string of bad luck, try wearing a bit of aventurine around your neck or carrying a piece in your pocket. During games of chance or gambling, try holding a piece of aventurine in your hand, or during those games when both hands are occupied, wear aventurine as a pendant near the skin.

Axe

Axes are lucky charms that can bring success. Archaeologists have unearthed talismans in the shape of axe heads in all parts of the world. They invariably have holes in them, indicating that they were worn around the neck. Ancient art from the Far East, pre-Columbian America, the Mediterranean, and Africa frequently depicts a double-bladed axe to indicate power.

Baby's Hair

When a mother cuts a lock of her baby's hair and puts it away for safekeeping, she is creating a lucky charm. From ancient times in cultures around the world, such mementos were intended to ensure a long and healthy life, as long as the lock of hair was kept in a safe place.

Bachelor's Button

In medieval Europe, where maidens often wore small bouquets of bachelor's buttons under their aprons for forty weeks to ensure luck in love, young men were encouraged to place the blue flowers in their pockets. According to the custom, the flower must be kept in the pocket for twenty-four hours. If it was dead after all that time in the dark, that was a sign that love would die, too, and the young man was probably doomed to an unhappy marriage. Obviously, it would have been impossible for the fragile flower to survive, and many a young man took the dead posy as a signal to stay single. And that may well be why they are called bachelor's buttons.

BADGER TOOTH

Serious gamblers believe that the tooth of a badger can bring good luck when sewn into their right-hand pocket.

BAMBOO

In India, a piece of bamboo with seven knots is part of an especially strong talisman believed capable of bringing both wisdom and power. The talisman consists of two circles with triangles drawn on them. The seven-knotted bamboo is placed across it and a representation of a snake is placed at right angles to it. The circles are a symbol of eternity, the triangles represent the Hindu Trinity (Brahma, the creator; Vishnu, the protector; and Siva, the destroyer). The snake stands for wisdom, and the bamboo represents the seven degrees of learning that are the foundation of the Hindu religion.

BARTHOLOMEW, SAINT

One of Christ's Apostles, Bartholomew is believed to have taken Christianity to India and Armenia, where he was martyred. His martyrdom was by flaying, which makes prayers to Saint Bartholomew important to the luck of tanners, shoemakers, bookbinders and others who work with leather.

Basil

In central Europe until a few generations ago, young girls wore sprigs of basil on their chests as a sign that they were virgins. Tradition had it that the basil would wither if a girl was not as advertised. On the other hand, it was also common for married women to wear basil in their hair as a means of perpetuating the love of their husbands.

In Elizabethan England, the herb served as a lucky charm for bachelors looking for a wife. It was customary for these swains to carry basil leaves in their pockets when courting because they were believed to attract sympathy. But if they should inadvertently pull the herb from their pocket in the presence of their love, it would attract scorn instead.

In Africa, basil is widely used to ward off bad spells and to cure traumatic shock. Some African people also carry basil as an antidote for scorpion bites.

A form of basil called tulashi was imported to America in the 1960s by the Hindu-inspired group known as "Hare Krishnas." This close relative of basil, common to India, is believed to bring luck to devotees of the sect. Sprigs of tulashi are kept in their homes on velvet cushions, and gifts of flowers and incense are presented to it every day to acknowledge the herb's luck-bringing qualities.

Bat

In Western cultures, where bats have been associated with witches since the Middle Ages, these flying mammals are generally considered bad luck, or at least no fun to have around. In many

parts of Europe, people believe that
ghosts take the form of bats and that
the places they inhabit are haunted.
But in China, bats are symbols of long
life, and representations of them worn as
lucky charms are guaranteed to bring happiness.

BEAD

The power of beads to bring good luck or to ward off bad
luck is among our most ancient beliefs. In general, beaded necklaces have been most commonly used to ward off the evil eye.
In most religions they have been used in worship because of a
very old belief that beads of glass or stone have occult power.
The type of stones strung together usually determines what kind
of luck the beads will bring. Amber, for instance, is believed to
have the power to cure a host of ailments when fashioned into
necklaces. Beads made of aquamarine can bring luck in love.
Onyx, believed to inspire deep thoughts, is usually used for
rosary beads in the Catholic church.

BEAN

Ancient tombs the world over have contained beans, either
real or as representations, because they were believed to contain the basic spark of life. The belief stems from the observa-
tion that beans kept in the dark for years will sprout when
they're brought back into the sun. The Egyptians believed that
beans were a symbol of immortality. The Romans thought they

had the power to repel ghosts. In medieval Europe, beans were worn to repel witches. In the southern United States, it is customary to eat black-eyed peas for luck on New Year's Eve. In many parts of Europe, a bean or a dried pea is baked inside a Christmas cake and the person who finds it in their piece can look forward to good luck all year long.

Bear

Among the natives of Siberia, the northern islands of Japan, and parts of Alaska, the bear is considered the luckiest of animals. Although hunters kill bears for food and for their fur, it is never done without prayers of apology, lest the killing bring bad luck. The animal is believed to have supernatural powers, probably because bears are able to hibernate through long winters without food or water.

Most of the tribes in the far north ritually kill a bear once each year in a ceremony they believe will ensure their good fortune. In Eastern Siberia, it is customary to lead the doomed bear through the village, visiting every household to bring luck to the family. Food is generally provided for the animal at every stop, but if the bear sniffs at the family larder instead, that is a sign of especially good fortune.

After the bear has been killed, its head is mounted on a tall pole as an amulet to bring luck to the entire village. Its power to produce luck lasts only until all of the flesh has decayed from it, after which it is given a solemn burial. Among some tribes, the skull is wedged into a tree stump and is believed to have the power to bring good fortune to the village until grass grows over it.

BEE

If a bee flies through your window, that's a sign of good luck. It is also a sign that a stranger will come to your door. But if the bee dies in your house, that means bad luck. So watch out for that stranger.

BEGINNER'S LUCK

No one who seriously believes in luck doubts for a minute that there is a special kind of luck reserved for beginners. One of mankind's oldest beliefs, possibly not without justification, is that anything new is just naturally better. And it follows that someone new at games of chance will usually do better the first time around. Eventually, of course, the law of averages will catch up with him, and even if his luck holds, it won't be as sweet as that first win.

In England, where they call soccer "football," and take it deadly seriously, the first warm-up move a team makes before a game is to pass the ball solemnly from the oldest to the youngest player, in hopes that beginner's luck will affect the whole team.

BELL

In ancient times all over the world, it was believed that evil spirits could put up with just about anything except the clanging of a bell. Over time, the bell itself, even when not ringing, came to be regarded as a powerful lucky symbol. Because it is suspended in a hanging position, it takes on the representation of all life suspended between heaven and earth. Its vault-like shape has become a symbol of heaven.

Bells are used in Christian churches as well as Hindu and Buddhist temples as a means of keeping evil away. The bell tolled at funerals is now explained as a signal to the living that a soul is passing to the other side and should be accompanied by prayers. But originally the tolling was intended to prevent evil forces from interfering with the soul's heavenward journey.

Bells are often used as warning of danger. Obviously, the fact they are easy to hear makes them perfect for the job. But just as important is the age-old belief in most European countries that the sound of a bell can turn away an approaching storm, deflect lightning or tame a tornado.

But why bells? Such things as gunpowder make more noise than bells, and the Chinese still routinely use it to frighten away harmful spirits. But after gunpowder was introduced into Europe, the English scientist Roger Bacon said he still thought bells were much better demon-chasers. In a thirteenth-century scientific report, Bacon concluded that it wasn't the sound of a bell in itself that had the power but the movement of the air caused by repeated tolling. In his opinion, it canceled out the turbulence caused by mischief-making spirits.

BERYL

Spheres of beryl were used in fifth-century Ireland to encourage healing, love, energy, and rain. This stone is similar to the aquamarine in that if worn when at sea, it is believed to provide protection from storms, drowning, and seasickness.

Beryl is said to have the peculiar ability to give its bearer the capacity to avoid being persuaded by unscrupulous salespersons or other conniving individuals. Hence, it allows the wearer to succeed in true love and to avoid attachments that seem convincing, but are lacking in true steadfastness. This stone is also given between lovers to intensify their bond, but can also be used to attract love as well as friendship.

If you are soon to be engaged in a debate, wear a piece of beryl so that you may be mannerly and congenial and gain the understanding of your opponent. If you have recently lost something, hold a piece of beryl in your hand, close your eyes, envision the object, and the stone's impression is said to depict the object's location. If you have a test or presentation coming up, wear beryl to focus your mind on the task at hand and to increase your ability to remember the information you are studying. Finally, if you are feeling lazy or lethargic, wear or hold a piece of beryl and concentrate on its energizing and focusing powers.

BIBIANA, SAINT

Bibiana was sainted for her martyrdom in Rome. She was a virgin who was killed there and then buried with her mother and sister who were also martyrs. A church was built on the site of their graves, and in the garden of that church an herb grew that had miraculous powers to cure epilepsy and headaches. It also substantially reduced the effects of overindulgence, or in modern terms, it relieved the effects of a hangover. Hence, almost 1,660 years after her death she is still invoked against epilepsy, headaches and hangovers.

BIRTHDAY CANDLES

Today when we place candles on a birthday cake and hope that we succeed in blowing them out with one breath so that we can receive our wish, we probably don't consider that this was an ancient worship ritual for the Greek goddess Artemis. Artemis was the goddess of the moon, marriage, and childbirth, and for the celebration of her birth, special cakes were formed in the shape of the moon and candles were placed on the temple altars. If worshipers blew out the candles in one breath, Artemis would watch over them and bring them good fortune, as well as make their wishes come true.

A similar custom began in Germany in the Middle Ages, when a cake was placed on the dinner table early in the morning of someone's birthday. It was surrounded by a circle of candles that burned throughout the day to ward off evil spirits. The candles were also a reminder that life is transitory and represented the candles that would one day be lighted for one's funeral. By blowing them out, the person celebrating the beginning of a new year of life is demonstrating the ability to control destiny. Blowing all of them out at one time is considered lucky because it implies more than just control, but mastery over one's fate.

BIRTHDAY SPANKINGS

A custom shared by virtually every child in America is the ritual of being spanked, one time for each year that has passed, on birthdays. The "whacks" are always followed by an extra one "for luck." Actually, each of the blows is intended to bring luck to the birthday child. The practice dates back to ancient rituals marking rites of passage. In cultures all over the world in ancient times, and in many places still prevalent today, initiation ceremonies follow a pattern of separation from the community and then a celebration of reentry. Birthday spankings are a kind of hazing, during which the honored person is singled out for a mild public humiliation, but is welcomed back to the party with that extra blow for luck.

BIRTHMARK

Although most of what we regard as lucky charms are things we can acquire, in the seventeenth century, moles and birthmarks were considered to be reliable signs of good and bad luck. Believers were quite certain that the marks held the key to an unalterable fate. Those who thought there was more good luck than bad in birthmarks made it a point to sprinkle black pepper on an expectant mother so her child would be born with plenty of them.

According to seventeenth-century lore, if you have a natural mark on top of your head, you will surely have another on the nape of your neck. The combination means that you are naturally witty and that your body is well formed. A mole in the center of the forehead is the sign of an industrious man or a fruitful woman. A mole or birthmark on the upper lip is a sign of great good fortune, and any above the chin indicates superiority over one's relatives. A small birthmark on a man's right arm is a sign of a compulsive gambler, but for a woman it means she will inherit great wealth.

Moles or birthmarks on the upper part of the body's left side predict long journeys. But more of them on the left side than the right will bring bad luck wherever you happen to go.

Black Cat

As superstitions go, the idea that black cats are unlucky is of fairly recent vintage. It dates back to the Middle Ages, when just about everybody believed in witches. They also believed a witch had the power to become a cat and that black was always the color of choice. It followed that if a black cat should cross your path, it just might be a witch in disguise and that could bring nothing but bad luck.

In ancient Egypt, however, all cats were sacred to the goddess Isis. Her daughter Bast, quite powerful in her own right, was represented as a cat. And among real felines, black ones were considered closest to an incarnation of the goddess herself. Anyone who killed one, accidentally or otherwise, usually paid for the transgression with his own life.

Sometimes a black cat can bring good luck. They are regarded as very lucky in Japan. American folk wisdom has it that if one comes to your door, it brings good fortune to the household. Sailors have long believed that a black cat aboard ship will ensure a safe voyage, and for generations sailors' wives have adopted black cats to help guarantee that their husbands will come home safe and sound.

BLAISE, SAINT

An early Christian bishop who was put to death by the Romans in A.D. 316, Saint Blaise was said to have performed miraculous cures, particularly in animals, during a long period when he lived as a hermit. Among his cures was of a boy who was choking to death on a fish bone. While Blaise was in prison awaiting execution, the boy's mother comforted him with food and candles. In eternal gratitude for this act of kindness, it is believed that Saint Blaise's influence can still help anyone suffering from sore throats.

BLARNEY STONE

If you visit Ireland, a visit to the ruins of Blarney Castle in County Cork will bring you a special kind of luck for the rest of your life. All you have to do is hang upside down with someone holding tightly to your heels and kiss the underside of a triangular piece of limestone known since 1446 as the Blarney Stone. Once you've kissed it, you can't help but be charming, and you'll be blessed with what many call the "gift of gab," but which the Irish simply call "blarney."

This is possible, according to the legend, because the original Lord of the Castle, Cormac MacCarthy, called on a Druid priestess to help him win a lawsuit. "Kiss a stone of your castle," she told him, "and sweet words will pour from your mouth." He did. And it worked. After he had saved his castle with his own eloquence, MacCarthy moved the stone so that kissing it would be nearly, but not quite, impossible. It was his way of making sure that his neighbors wouldn't share his gift and take him to court again.

BLOODSTONE

Considered an especially lucky charm for soldiers going into battle, the bloodstone was worn on the thumbs of ancient Egyptian men to give them courage. In India's early civilizations, the stone was soaked in water and applied to wounds to stop bleeding. The red-flecked stone is also considered very lucky for farmers and for breeders of cattle.

For luck in business dealings, bloodstone, a green stone flecked with red spots, is useful, since the main powers it projects are courage, strength, wealth, power, legal success, business success, and power. This stone has been considered magical for over three thousand years and was particularly popular with the Babylonians, who carried it to defeat their enemies and to open doors. Since bloodstone is reputed to be effective in checking bleeding, soldiers often carried it with them into battle, and today it is still used to maintain physical health and to alleviate diseases of the blood. Some athletes wear the stone to boost their physical strength and to extend their life spans.

Because of the distinctive green coloring of bloodstone, it is associated with money, wealth, and business. If you own a business of your own or deal with cash transactions, you could try placing a piece of bloodstone in the cash register to encourage a steady flow of money into, and not out of, the register. Also, try carrying a piece of bloodstone in your pocket or wearing a piece as a pendant in order to attract wealth.

BROOMSTICK

Although it is hard for us to think of a witch without a broomstick, the Gypsies say that if a witch is seen near your house, you can protect yourself by placing a broomstick across the threshold, forming the shape of a cross. No witch, or any other form of evil, will be able to pass over it.

BULL'S HEAD

The ancient Etruscans put great store in talismans engraved with representations of the head of a bull. It brought long life and good health and, they believed, success in love. The Egyptians considered the bull to be an emblem of strength and dignity. The ancient Greeks regarded the bull as the earthly form of a god who insured fertility, not only on their farms, but in themselves. Representations of bull's heads in their jewelry were intended to let the god know that they honored him; by wearing the symbol, they would be rewarded with large families and productive fields.

BURNING EAR

In times past, as well as today, people believed that when the ear is burning, someone is talking or gossiping about the sufferer. This idea originated from the belief that even when people were at great distances, they could still be heard. The older superstition specified that if your right ear was burning, someone was speaking of you in a spiteful manner, and if your left ear was burning, someone was speaking of you in a loving manner.

Vengeance could be exacted on the gossiper, too. When the right ear was burning, you could pinch your own ear, and the person who was speaking ill of you would bite his tongue and stop speaking.

C

CADUCEUS

The wand of Mercury, associated in our day with the medical profession, has been a lucky talisman for thousands of years. Before the doctors appropriated it, the caduceus was worn by people who wanted the gift of eloquence and eternal youth. The staff itself was said to have been given to Mercury, the gods' messenger, by the god of light, Apollo. It consisted of a magic wand topped by a pinecone, the symbol of healing, and wings with the power to direct human thoughts to a higher plane. Anyone who carried it, Apollo said, would have the power to settle arguments with the gift of speech. Mercury, the story goes, took the wand out for a test and came upon two serpents fighting one another. He placed it between them and talked them out of their dispute.

From that time, the entwined serpents became part of the wand itself. They symbolize regeneration, because snakes shed and regrow their skins, and remind us that we can shed our lower nature and rise to new heights. Although the story suggests that the talisman is a gift from the Greeks, the same symbol has been found on stone tablets unearthed in India. A ceremonial cup with a similar staff dating back to 2600 B.C. was found among artifacts left behind by the Mesopotamians.

CALCITE

Love, peace, purification, energy, and spirituality are all powers contained in calcite. Perhaps its most useful aspect is its ability to double the power of the intention the bearer places on the stone.

Pink calcite is often held in the hand to calm and soothe, and it is also used to attract and maintain a love relationship. Blue calcite is strongly connected to healing activities, and green calcite draws money and prosperity. Orange calcite gives the body an extra energy boost when held in the hand.

If you are currently experiencing an illness or have recently recovered from sickness, try placing blue calcite between two blue or purple candles to feel its purifying effect. If you are searching for monetary prosperity, try surrounding a piece of green calcite with lit green candles each morning and money should follow.

CANDLE

No one knows when candles were invented or by whom. But there is evidence that they were used as early as 3000 B.C. both in Egypt and in Crete to frighten away evil spirits.

The ancient Hebrews used candles to repel evil influences from the dying, and after death, candles were kept burning for a week. This custom still exists in the Jewish ritual known as Shiva, during which family members are sequestered for a week after the death of a loved one. Another similar custom, intended to keep evil influences away from the deceased as well as the survivors, is found in Ireland, where twelve candles are placed in a circle around a coffin. Three candles are sometimes burned at Irish wakes and their wicks are saved as a treatment for burns.

Because of the association of three candles with wakes, the Irish consider it bad luck for three candles to be burned in a room at the same time. The belief also extends to the theater, where actors and others regard three candles as a sign of impending bad luck.

In Scotland, candles are burned for luck at times of serious illness or death. In order to bring luck, these candles must be secured from a person regarded as unlucky, such as a witch.

In the Appalachians, a fluttering candle flame is a sign that bad luck will follow. Similarly, the Scotch-Irish believe that a candle burning in an empty room will result in bad luck. In Britain, a candle whose wax drips around it rather than straight down is a predictor that bad luck is just around the corner. In Germany, it is believed that bad luck will follow if a candle wick divides in two and burns with two flames. In nearby Austria, on the other hand, such an event is considered a sign that good news is about to arrive in the mail.

In Shakespeare's *King Richard the Third*, the Ghost of Buckingham enters a room filled with blue candlelight, reflecting an old English belief that a candle burning with a blue flame brings nothing but trouble. This bad luck can be avoided, though, by extinguishing the candle under running water.

In the seventeenth century, it was believed that burning a candle that had been consecrated in a church would force a pirate to reveal the resting place of buried treasure if its light were reflected in his eyes.

CARBUNCLE

"Carbuncle" is an old term for a large red gemstone, most frequently a garnet, that has been cut with a convex or flat back and a smooth domed surface. The ancients referred to the carbuncle as the "luminous stone," and believed it had the power to collect light by day and release it by night. One tradition holds that Noah took a carbuncle with him to light his way on his famous voyage. Muslims believe that wearing one into battle will protect a soldier from wounds. In many parts of Europe, the stone is still regarded as protection against infection as well as wounds. And many believe that a charm containing a carbuncle will dispel evil thoughts, lift your spirits, discourage arguments, bring success in business, and even settle indigestion.

CARNELIAN

In India, where this red, translucent, hard stone related to quartz is most abundant, it is believed that carnelian in rings or seals has the power to ward off almost any evil. It is especially effective in preventing fevers.

CAT'S-EYE

The stone known as a cat's-eye, sometimes the luckiest shooter in a youngster's bag of marbles, was once believed effective in preventing all diseases of the chest and throat. In India, it is common wisdom that if one carries a cat's-eye stone, fortune will never diminish. Among gamblers, it is a charm of choice to bring luck in games of chance.

CAUL

The thin membrane that protects unborn babies, called the caul, sometimes remains covering the head of a newborn. The ancient Romans believed that children born with a caul were blessed with uncommon good luck. These children, they thought, were protected for life from drowning. It was also believed that they had the power to predict the future and the ability to converse with unseen spirits.

Over the centuries midwives collected and preserved cauls, which they sold as amulets. Sailors were among their most frequent customers because of the belief that wearing one around the neck was a guarantee against drowning. Among certain Native American tribes, it was believed that a caul shriveled and turned to dust at the moment of death. These same people believed that if one's preserved caul was ripped or torn, death was imminent and unavoidable.

In medieval Italy, people who had been born with cauls and wore them as talismans were called *benandanti* (good walkers), and were relied upon to do battle with witches and demons at planting time. It was believed that they were capable of assuming the shapes of animals, as witches also were, and they went out in the dark of night to encounter the forces of evil. The weapon of the benandanti was stalks of fennel, while the demons fought with stalks of sorghum. If the good walkers were victorious in the all-night battle, a good harvest was guaranteed. If the forces of evil won, crops were considered doomed and it was believed a famine would follow.

CHALCEDONY

A type of quartz that unlike others is not crystalline but is translucent and waxy, chalcedony has been used in charms and amulets for centuries to prevent visions that come in the night as well as general sadness. The ancient Egyptians usually used chalcedony on their scarabs.

CHAMPAGNE

This wine is often used in rituals to ensure good luck on a voyage or in the initial stages of a new endeavor. Champagne is considered a very lucky wine that is used in the celebrations of childbirth, baptism, marriage, and the launching of a ship.

Today the champagne bottle smashed against the side of a ship as it sets sail on its maiden voyage is a substitution for the earlier tradition of making a human or animal sacrifice to appease the sea gods. Also, the name that the ship is given during the champagne christening must never be changed or it will bring extremely bad luck.

CHANGING WOMAN

Among the rituals of nearly every religion in the history of mankind, the most common are those marking the coming of age of young men and women. Among the Apache of the

American Southwest, the transformation of a girl into a woman was accomplished in a long ceremony during which the girl was believed to absorb the spirit of a goddess known as the "changing woman," whose presence among them brought good fortune to the entire community. At the end of the ceremony, the medicine man picked up a basket filled with coins, corn kernels and bits of candy and dumped it over the girl's head. The offerings were then picked up by the assembled spectators, who treasured them as charms that would bring them wealth and an abundance of food. The newly initiated woman was believed to be possessed by the changing woman for the following four days, during which time it was considered very good luck to touch her.

CHARM

In modern use, the word *charm* is frequently used to describe an amulet or talisman. But originally, it was something that brought good luck when combined with a gesture or a chant. Charms also could cure or prevent an illness or affliction.

Mark Twain's Tom Sawyer turned an ordinary bean into a charm that could remove warts. His formula was to cut the wart and dab a bit of blood from it onto a bean. Then he recommended burying the bean at midnight in the dark of the moon. It wouldn't work, he claimed, unless you said "Down bean; off wart; come no more to bother me" while burying it.

Among the oldest of charms is a smooth stone that has been exposed to the light of a full moon for three nights. Wearing such a stone around your neck can make you the picture of health. Our ancestors also believed that a stone with a natural hole in it is a powerful charm to counteract the influence of witches and fairies.

CHEATING FATE

Beliefs in an unalterable fate can sometimes make a person miserable. The natives of Madagascar believe that anyone born in November during the rainy season is doomed to a life of sorrow. To prevent this, they simply remove the cover from a pot of boiling water and sprinkle the drops of condensed moisture onto the child's cheeks. These symbolic tears will, it is hoped, be enough to prevent real tears from falling during the baby's lifetime.

CHERRY TREE

It is very good luck to have a cherry tree shading your house—which is probably why George Washington's father was so upset when the young future president took an axe to one. It is also said that lovers who meet for the first time under a cherry tree will be very lucky together. Charms in the shape of cherries are considered a lucky gift from a close friend. But be careful: If you pick cherry blossoms in the spring, you may have bad luck all summer long.

CHESTNUT

Carrying a chestnut in your pocket will not only bring you luck, but in many parts of the world it is believed that it can cure a headache, get rid of a backache, and bring relief from chest pains.

CHRISTOPHER, SAINT

Saint Christopher, originally named Offero, is the patron saint of travelers. A hermit who taught him the ways of Christianity told him to live near a river and carry people across, which is how he became associated with travel. The tale is told that one night, he had the task of carrying a small infant across the river who became more and more heavy as they moved. The child revealed himself as Jesus Christ and told Offero that his new name would be Christopher, which means "Christ-bearer" in Greek.

Jesus also told him to return to the other side of the river and plant his staff in the ground, where it would bear fruit the next day. Christopher went on to preach the gospel and eventually be arrested because he would not sacrifice to the Roman gods. He was sentenced to die by fire and arrows, neither of which harmed him. He was finally martyred and is venerated today as a protector of travelers.

In the Middle Ages, Saint Christopher was often prayed to for protection against storms and plagues, and in order to protect travelers from calamity. In the twentieth century, he is widely called upon to protect travelers on the road and in the air. Similarly, a church in Paris dedicated to him is based on the idea that anyone who sees Saint Christopher's image will not die that day. Paintings and pictures of the saint are often placed near the exit of the church so that all in attendance will be sure to see them and be protected from death for that day.

CHRYSANTHEMUM

Japan's national flower is considered a symbol of the perfection of the human spirit. For thousands of years it has been the emblem of the emperor. In the fourteenth century, during one of Japan's many internal wars, every warrior in the emperor's service wore a chrysanthemum into battle to bring courage. The emperor's men won the war.

CHRYSOLITE

This stone, frequently confused with the topaz, comes in many colors, each variety having its own name. Some green forms are called olivine; when it is emerald green, it is sometimes called a peridot. By any name, chrysolite has been a lucky charm for thousands of years. Just owning one, some of our ancestors believed, would give one special occult powers. In a gold setting as a ring or a necklace, chrysolite could dispel nightmares. It was also believed effective in giving its owner the gift of gab and could cure stuttering and all other speech impediments.

CHRYSOPRASE

This is an all-around good-luck stone and an excellent aid in the pursuit of happiness. Chrysoprase is a mint-green stone with particular powers in luck, happiness, companionship, healing, and prosperity. It is also effective in creating good cheer and eradicating miserliness, stress, envy, and selfishness.

Chrysoprase is mainly used in order to gain increased happiness, but also helps in the acquisition of eloquence, successes in novel endeavors, and in making new friends. Mainly, chrysoprase can be used to ward off any form of negativity and unhappiness. It can additionally help to strengthen eyesight and make the blood more capable of resisting disease.

If you are in need of good humor or a decrease in an irritatingly high level of stress, try carrying a small piece of chrysoprase with you wherever you go.

CIRCLE

The circle is one of mankind's oldest symbols of good fortune. It stands for eternity because it is without beginning or end. It is a sign of completeness, perfection, and wholeness. The idea probably began as a representation of the apparent path of the sun around the earth. Our ancestors were careful to move in a clockwise direction, following the sun's east-west path. Today, many people think that bad luck can be averted by turning clockwise three times.

Over time, people began to believe that evil spirits could not cross a circle because it represented a greater power than theirs, that of the sun. The concept gave us many kinds of lucky symbols, including rings of every description and the circular designs of Amish hex signs, not to mention the wreaths we hang on our doors at Christmastime. Lucky charms such as horseshoes and wishbones are also rooted in the idea of the power of circles. Although open at one end, they are believed capable of trapping evil spirits within themselves. The opening serves as an entry point, important because while witches and other bad spirits can't get out of a circle, they can't get into one, either.

The ability of circles to thwart such spirits also led to the custom of painting one's lips red. The ancients believed that evil could get into the body through the mouth, and they counteracted the possibility by painting a red circle around it. Hoopshaped earrings were also developed as the same kind of lucky charm because their circular shapes protected the opening of the ear.

CLARE, SAINT

If your favorite television program seems doomed to cancellation, a little luck might come its way through the influence of Saint Clare, who was officially declared the patron saint of television in 1958. This may seem odd because Clare died at Assisi in 1253 and spent her entire life in a convent, where, even if it had been invented by then, television would certainly have been forbidden. The association with TV came from one of the legends about her, which says she once witnessed every detail of a Christmas mass, even though an illness prevented her from going to the cathedral in person.

Coal

Children are often warned that if they aren't good, they'll probably find lumps of coal in their Christmas stockings. But in some parts of the world, it is considered quite lucky to find a piece of coal in the street, or to be given one by a friend. In Northern England, it is customary to place little piles of coal on doorsteps on the last day of the year. Each person who enters the house on New Year's Eve picks up one of the lumps and carries it inside to bring good luck to the household.

Coin

There aren't many people who can pass a fountain or a wishing well without tossing a coin into the water for luck. It is a tradition that dates back to the ancient Greeks and possibly even further into antiquity. The ancients believed that a gift of a little money to the gods who inhabited their wells would keep the wells from running dry. They and others also believed that the gods of the sea, who could do a lot of damage if they were offended, could be kept happy if a few coins were occasionally thrown their way as a tribute. It was more convenient, and just as acceptable to the gods, to throw coins into fountains as into the sea itself. A custom observed all over the world says that if you look for your reflection in the water and then make a wish after throwing a coin into it, the wish will be granted. But when in Rome, remember that their sea gods will accept no less than three coins.

Many people consider it lucky to carry a coin with their birth date. Some say that coins found heads-up are also lucky, and that a coin minted in a leap year will bring good fortune. Luckiest of all are coins that are bent or have holes in them, especially if they turn up as change after making a purchase. The luck of such coins is enhanced if they are carried in a left-hand pocket or worn around the neck.

Coins can bring luck in literally hundreds of ways. You'll have good luck if you keep a jar of pennies in the kitchen. The first coin you receive each day should be placed in an otherwise empty pocket and it will attract more for you. A coin in a new coat or jacket, handbag, or wallet will bring good luck. If you get pennies as change on a Monday, you'll have good luck all week long.

In the tenth century, a crusader named Sir Simon Lockhart went home to Scotland from the Holy Land with a blood-red stone attached to a silver coin. Known as the Lee Penny, it was said to be able to cure rabies and ailments in cattle. At one point, the people of Newcastle put up a bond nearly equal to the city's whole treasury to stop a plague. It worked. But five hundred years later a descendant of the crusader, Sir James Lockhart, who had inherited the Lee Penny, was arrested on charges of witchcraft when he used the coin to cure diseased cattle. The court was told that he did it "without using any words, such as charmers and sorcerers do." He was acquitted, but warned to be more careful in the future, and the Lee Penny was hidden away, never to use its power again.

Color

Colors can influence more than your mood. Each color has a special significance in attracting, or repelling, the power of the planets.

BLACK

Saturn is attracted by black, and because Saturn has a negative effect on children, youngsters are cautioned never to wear black clothing. It is a good color, however, for persons born under the signs of Libra, Aquarius, or Capricorn.

BLUE

The color associated with Venus as well as the color of the sky, blue has been sacred in religions dating back to prehistoric times. Today it is associated with the Virgin Mary. We sometimes say we are "blue" when we are less than happy. Still, blue is a happy, even lucky color for most of us. And when we have unexpected good luck, we often say it came "out of the blue." It is an especially lucky color for people born under the signs of Aquarius, Libra, and Taurus.

Blue neckbands have been worn for centuries by nursing mothers in parts of Europe. They believe the color protects their babies from fevers. And what bride would tempt fate by walking down the aisle without "something borrowed, something blue"?

BROWN

Not generally considered a lucky color except in very light shades. Those born under the sign of Cancer are advised to avoid brown altogether.

GREEN

One of the most common theatrical superstitions is that green should be avoided at all costs. The tradition began in the days when stages were lit by limelights, which burned lime, producing a greenish light that made anything green nearly invisible. In the Middle Ages, it was believed that green was the color of fairies and other "little people" who didn't like the idea of sharing it with mere mortals. In Ireland, leprechauns notwithstanding, green is considered the luckiest of colors. It is also a lucky color for those born under the signs of Aquarius and Capricorn.

PURPLE

Considered the color of royalty since the ancient Phoenicians extracted purple dye from sea creatures and sold it around the world at incredibly high prices, purple is an exceptionally good color for anyone who wants to get lucky—especially people born under the sign of Pisces or Sagittarius.

RED

People born under the sign of Libra or Taurus may find red an unlucky color, but those whose birth date falls in Aries or Scorpio should wear red for good luck. The ancients believed that a talisman written in red was doubly powerful. In China and other parts of the East, no other color has as much power to bring good luck.

WHITE

The classic color of purity, white (or silver) is especially lucky for people born under the sign of Cancer, Gemini or Virgo. Though in some cultures, a white horse, a white cat or a white mouse are all considered very unlucky, in general, white can bring you good luck.

YELLOW

As the color associated with the sun, yellow or gold is lucky for just about everyone. People born under the sign of Virgo or Taurus might disagree. It can bring them misfortune, some say. But it is the lucky color of Leo.

CONFETTI

As the bride and groom exit the church after being married, it is traditional to throw confetti or rice over them as a celebratory gesture. In the past, however, wheat was thrown, but only over the bride in order to ensure fertility and an abundance of children. The idea was for the bride to produce children as abundantly as wheat produces bread. Wedding cake is also a symbol of fertility. Guests of the wedding used to present "bride-cakes" to the new bride in order to encourage a fertile union.

COPPER BRACELET

Anyone who suffers the pain of arthritis might consider wearing a copper bracelet to ease it. Many people who don't have arthritis wear them anyway as a lucky charm to prevent the crippling disease. Although the sufferers may swear by them, and the others are certain they'd be doubled over in pain without their copper bracelets, there is no scientific evidence that the charm works. But even without the blessing of the medical community, people have relied on copper bracelets since the Middle Ages, long before aspirin and other modern painkillers arrived. Best of all, copper has no side effects!

CORAL

Coral, especially if it is red, has been regarded for centuries as a powerful material for amulets. The ancient Romans believed coral could keep witches and demons away. In many later cultures, it was considered perfect for warding off the evil eye. The Egyptians crushed it and spread it over their fields to keep locusts away. Some people believe that a piece of coral over a bed can prevent nightmares, and many think that coral anywhere in the house protects them from domestic arguments. In China, a coral amulet protects the wearer against insanity.

CORNELIUS, SAINT

One of the early popes, who was exiled after a disagreement over welcoming repentant sinners back into the Christian fold, Saint Cornelius is said to be able to bring relief to those who suffer from earaches, epilepsy, fever and twitching. This belief stems from the harshness of his exile.

CORNERSTONE

Even buildings made of steel and glass usually have a cornerstone, often engraved with the date construction began and filled with things important to the building's original owner. It is a talisman intended to bring luck not only during construction, but throughout the life of the building. The custom has its origins in prehistoric times, when it was believed the gods must be compensated for the land a structure occupies. Originally a sacrifice, often human, was offered, but eventually it became common to put money or other valuables inside or under the first stone laid.

Corno

In Italy and among Italian-Americans, a charm in the shape of a horn, known as a corno, is frequently worn as a powerful bringer of luck. Although associated with good luck in general, it was originally intended as a means of protection against the evil eye. The most powerful cornos are made from actual horns of rams, bulls or oxen, but other pointed natural objects such as pig's teeth, rooster spurs and crab claws are also often used. Many are made from gold, silver or coral, and sometimes those made from horn are embellished with gold and silver, not to enhance their power, but to call attention to the affluence of the wearer.

Mounted on a wall, horns can protect and bring luck to a place of business or a home. But the most common cornos are those that are worn as a necklace or carried as a pocket piece. After all, one can always use luck.

After bright red chilies were introduced to Europe from South America in the sixteenth century, people noticed that they closely resembled the traditional shape of their cornos and began using chilies as a substitute. This was especially true in cities such as Naples, where natural horns were not always easy to find. In our time, these so-called chili-cornos are commonly made of plastic and carried as lucky charms. Sometimes embellished with the crest of an Italian city, the bright red, stubby-pointed charms are carried as watch fobs or key chains. They also turn up hanging over rear-view mirrors of cars as a way of bringing luck to the driver. Many truck drivers sport these charms because they believe they will ensure their safety while driving at high speeds. The plastic chili-cornos are also frequently seen in the casinos of Las Vegas and Atlantic City, where they are among the most popular lucky charms of gamblers.

CORNUCOPIA

A silver representation of the horn of plenty worn by the owner of a business will make that business thrive. The same charm is also helpful to expectant mothers because it not only promotes a safe delivery, but helps guarantee a healthy, bouncing baby. The original cornucopia was a goat's horn given by the god Jupiter to his nurse for having taken such good care of him as a baby. It was magic and for the rest of her life the nurse was able to take anything from inside the horn simply by wishing for it.

Cottonwood Tree

Among the Sioux Indians of the Great Plains, the cotton-wood tree, which they call the "sacred rustling tree," is one of the earthly representations of Wakan-Taka, the Great Spirit. As such, it has the power to bring luck to people who treat it with the proper respect. The tree is used in many tribal ceremonies and when one is cut down to be used in a ritual, great care is taken to keep it from touching the ground before it can be erected in the ceremonial place.

Cottonwood trunks are always used as the centerpiece of sacred lodges. The poles that form the outer walls and those that become the roof, also always of cottonwood, are always twenty-eight in number. The Sioux believe that four and seven are lucky numbers. Multiplied together, the even luckier number is twenty-eight. The ancestors of the Sioux confirmed the mystical power of this number by observing that the life of the moon is twenty-eight days. Similarly, they observed that the life-giving buffalo has twenty-eight ribs. No Sioux warrior ever went into battle without a war bonnet consisting of twenty-eight feathers, no more, no less.

Crescent

Among the most powerful of all lucky symbols, the crescent is especially lucky for young children and their mothers. In ancient Egypt, the crescent moon was the symbol of Isis, the mother of the gods. As its symbolism spread throughout the world, it

eventually became a symbol of paradise, especially when represented with a star. It is particularly significant in Islam. The crescent became important to the cultures of the Middle East when
the Turks conquered the Byzantine capital of Constantinople in
A.D. 330 and established the Ottoman Empire. Among the
spoils of war was a statue of Hecate, a later incarnation of Isis,
whose crescent symbol had protected the city for generations
before they arrived. Already familiar with the crescent, they
adopted it as the protector of their empire, which lasted more
than 1,500 years.

CRICKET

A cricket on the hearth has been a sign of household luck
for thousands of years. And the idea is prevalent in every corner
of the world. Possibly the belief stems from prehistoric times,
when a cricket's chirping provided a kind of companionship. The
cricket has also served as a watchdog in China and other Asian
countries for generations. At any sign of danger, the chirping will
stop. Almost every Native American tribe believed in the cricket
as a bringer of luck, and they regarded imitating the sound a
cricket makes as disrespectful. In the Far East as well as across
Europe, it is considered very bad luck to kill a cricket, even by
accident. Images of crickets appear on charms and amulets, particularly those intended to ward off the evil eye, in most ancient
cultures of the Middle East and Europe. One of the best-known
in America is the large weather vane on Boston's Fanuel Hall, a
copper cricket fashioned by our Colonial forefathers to protect
the building.

CROSS

Although the cross has come to be a symbol of Christianity, it was venerated both as a religious and lucky sign for centuries before the Christian era. It has been found in parts of the world where the message of Christianity never reached. The Aztecs in pre-Columbian Mexico regarded it as a symbol of the rain god, the most important in their pantheon. In most primitive religions, the cross represents the tree of life. In some ancient cultures, the crosspiece intersecting the upright represented a ladder that helped a worshiper to reach God. In other cultures, the upright pointed the way to heaven and the crosspiece represented earthly influences. The oldest known version of the cross, dating back to prehistory and found all over the world, including among the Native Americans, is the swastika. This cross with its arms folded back took on a sinister meaning in the 1930s when Adolf Hitler adopted it as the symbol of his Nazi party. It wasn't a choice he made lightly. Hitler was very conscious of the power of lucky charms and it was his intention to crown his ambition with what he considered the luckiest charm of all. Fortunately for the world, it didn't work. But if Hitler didn't succeed in bringing the world under his heel, he managed to turn it away from a symbol that had been considered lucky almost from the time that man began to walk upright.

CROSSING FINGERS

Among the best ways to avert bad luck when you don't have a lucky charm handy is to cross your fingers. The power of such an act dates back to the early Christians who were forced to worship in secret. While they couldn't have representations of the cross to inspire them, they could, and did, create a reminder of Christ's passion by making a cross of their middle and index fingers.

CROW

At the Tower of London, six ravens are kept fed and preened because of a legend that says if they should ever decide to fly away, the Tower's walls will crumble. Their close cousins, the crows, aren't quite so welcome. For centuries, farmers have erected crosses in their fields to drive away the evil spirits that crows were thought to represent. As further insurance, the crosses were draped with cloth that would flutter in the breeze and unnerve the birds. Eventually, the crosses took on human form as scarecrows. But the birds can bring you good luck. If you see one flying, your wish will come true as long as the crow does not flap its wings before going out of sight. If it should, the wish might still be granted if you cover your eyes. If the bird is nowhere in sight when you uncover them, you'll get your wish.

DAISY

Little girls everywhere pull away the petals of daisies, reciting "he loves me, he loves me not" with each one. The luckiest of them has chosen a daisy with an odd number of petals so that the last one will be an affirmation of love. Gypsies believe that a girl can recover an absent lover by sleeping with daisy root under her pillow.

DAVID, SAINT

The patron saint of Wales, Saint David is also affectionately known as "Taffy," for his name in the Welsh language, "Dafydd." It is considered a wish for good luck when a Welshman is addressed by this name. Nearly everyone in Wales believes that they will have luck in the coming year if they wear either a leek or a daffodil on his feast-day, March 1.

DAYS OF THE WEEK

Is today your lucky day? Any day can be. But the day you were born can have as much influence on the luck of your life as the star you were born under.

SUNDAY

Born on the first day of the week, you probably have an optimistic outlook on life. It is said that your luck, generally good, will be even better if you wear gold. Sunday is also a lucky day for people born under the sign of Leo.

MONDAY

Silver charms, especially crescents, will bring you luck if you were born on a Monday. You are likely to have an active imagination, and people find you attractive.

TUESDAY

You'll find luck in wearing red if your birth date was on Tuesday. You are enthusiastic about life and have a great influence over others. If you were born under the signs of Aeries or Scorpio, Tuesday is your lucky day.

WEDNESDAY

If you were born in the middle of the week, blue is your lucky color and jewelry with blue stones should always be set in silver. You get along extremely well with all kinds of people. If your birth date is in the sign of Aquarius, Gemini, or Virgo, Wednesday is your lucky day.

THURSDAY

A Thursday baby will grow up with an overpowering love of travel and the adventure of discovering new places. When you go, be sure to wear a charm representing an ankh or a cross of some kind for good luck on your journey. People born under the sign of Sagittarius can expect good luck to come their way on Thursday.

FRIDAY

If you were born on a Friday, you'll be very lucky in love. Diamonds are your best friend and they are sure to bring you luck in everything you do. Friday is among the luckiest of all days, considered auspicious for people born under four different astrological signs: Cancer, Libra, Pisces and Taurus. Possibly that is why so many agree with the expression, "Thank God it's Friday!"

SATURDAY

Born on a Saturday, you are likely to be a workaholic. But you don't mind. You know that hard work pays off. You can increase your luck at work by wearing a charm in the form of an hourglass. But you'll also find a gold watch a luck-bringer, unlikely as that may seem. It is a lucky day for Capricorns.

DEATH OMENS

In the world of luck, nothing is quite as unlucky as death itself. Although it is obviously unavoidable, every culture around the world has its own unique omens that predict death is just around the corner.

In many places, these omens occur in nature, such as unusual cloud formations or uncommon storms. In England, it is believed that coffin-shaped cinders on the family hearth mean that death will visit the family soon. Certain animals, insects and birds are also associated with impending death. Blackbirds and those that fly by night, such as owls, rooks, ravens and crows, are among them. Dogs, which in ancient mythology were the guardians of the underworld, predict death through long unexplained barking, especially in the dead of night. In parts of Europe, it is believed that if the firstborn lamb in the spring is black, the shepherd will experience a death in the family before the following spring.

DEER

Among the Chinese, a talisman engraved with the head of a stag or deer will bring success in any profession where study and research are important, such as writing or the law.

DEMON QUELLER

In Japan and in parts of China, on the fifth day of the fifth month each year, families with male children under the age of seven celebrate what is known as the Boys' Festival, which brings long life and good luck to their sons. The carp, an ancient symbol of strength and virility as well as of good luck, is the festival's primary symbol. But as powerful a luck-bringer as the carp is, it is not considered quite enough to protect these young boys who represent a family's most valuable asset.

It is believed that at this particular time, they are especially vulnerable to the influence of demons who bring nothing but bad luck. To protect them, and to bring them good luck, images of Shoki, the demon queller, are painted on banners that are unfurled outside the homes of these vulnerable children. Shoki, a large, bearded man carrying an enormous sword, first appeared in Chinese folklore in the eighth century. According to the story, a demon managed to get into the emperor's bedchamber, snatched up his jade flute and his consort's perfume bag and began dancing around the room. Suddenly, Shoki appeared out of nowhere, snatched up the demon, poked its eyes out and then ate it. Demons have been terrified of this creature ever since.

The emperor's benefactor identified himself as a scholar who had committed suicide a century and a half earlier after failing his civil service exams, a crucial test for young men in the Confucian world. The emperor, relieved to have escaped with his life, ordered the man's body transferred to a consecrated grave and in return secured the ghost's promise that he would spend eternity ridding the world of demons.

Although Shoki is a lucky spirit to have around, Chinese artists have frequently represented him as a drunkard who relies on demons to lead him from place to place. And in Japan, artists have often portrayed the demon queller as being quelled himself by beautiful courtesans. But the banners hung out during the Boys' Festival always portray him as a heroic figure. This is no time to offend the spirit who has the power to ensure good luck.

DENIS, SAINT

The patron saint of France, and the first bishop of Paris, was executed on the hill known as Montmartre (hill of the martyrs) in A.D. 250. According to the legend, Saint Denis picked up his own head and carried it to his burial place, the present site of the abbey of Saint Denis, some distance away. Because of this act, it is considered lucky to pray to him for anyone suffering from headaches. His memory is also believed to have a good effect for anyone suffering from strife or frenzy.

DIAMOND

Officers in the Roman legions wore diamond amulets on their left arm to guarantee victory in battle. For centuries, women wore diamond necklaces to avoid the evil eye. In our day, diamonds are symbols of luck among those engaged to be married. In fact, no one would ever think of a diamond as anything but lucky.

But as far as diamonds are concerned, luck is a relative thing. The bigger the stone, it is said, the less luck it will bring. If it's too big, in fact, it's more likely to produce bad luck. A case in point is the biggest blue diamond in the world, the 44.5-carat Hope diamond. It was said to have been stolen from the forehead of an Indian idol and taken to France, where it became part of the crown jewels of King Louis XIV. Although he himself can hardly be considered an unlucky monarch, his mistress, Mme. de Montespan, acquired the stone and died soon afterward. Later it was given to Marie Antoinette, who was guillotined. In 1830, it was bought by Thomas Hope, an English banker whose family quickly fell on hard times. Subsequent owners included Jacques Colet, a suicide; Prince Ivan Kanitovitsky, murdered; Sultan Abdul Hamed, dethroned; and Simon Montharides, whose entire family was killed in an accident. The Hope diamond was eventually bought for $40,000 in 1907 by Texan Evalyn Walsh McLean, whose husband, son, and daughter all died soon after she brought it to America. Her only surviving heir died mysteriously in 1967. Later, the stone was donated to the Smithsonian Institution, which has it on display at Washington's Museum of Natural History.

Dolphin

Cities that owe their existence to the sea, such as New York and Amsterdam, abound in carvings of dolphins, which are not just decorative, but are intended to bring luck to the port itself. The belief stems from the fact that ancient sailors who spent months or even years out of sight of land found the sight of dolphins swimming around their ships to be the first sign that land was near. As a lucky charm, a representation of a dolphin has long been believed to be especially effective in bringing good fortune to artists and musicians.

Domovik

In Russia, many people believe their home inhabited by a spirit called a domovik. It is usually perceived as the ghost of the founder of the family and is regarded as its protector and bringer of good luck. He is represented as a bearded old man and is always referred to as "Grandfather" or simply "He." It is considered bad luck to give a domovik a proper name.

The spirit lives behind the kitchen stove, and when a family moves into a new house, fire from the old stove is the first thing moved so that the domovik will feel welcome in his new surroundings. In addition to securing luck for the family, the domovik also helps them with small household chores. Though a generally friendly spirit, he can become displeased, at which time he makes disturbing noises and sometimes violently rearranges the furniture. Some domoviks have been known to become severely angry, and have vented their displeasure by burning the house down.

DOORS

In many places around the world, it is considered bad luck to enter a house through the back door. In parts of Europe, circles are drawn on doors, both front and back, to keep evil influences from entering a house. Many people also paint patterns on doorsteps for the same purpose. These markings are usually intricate patterns of unbroken lines. In central Europe, it is customary to slam a door several times when closing it. In this way, ghosts and evil spirits trying to get in will be trapped between the door and its frame. In superstitious English households, when death occurs, the doors are removed from their hinges and rehung in the opposite direction to prevent the spirit from returning.

EARRING

Originally developed as a means of protecting the ears from the effects of the evil eye and other dangers lurking in the air, earrings have other uses as amulets. Sailors, who for generations were the only men who could wear them without attracting a raised eyebrow, believed that they could prevent drowning. Because they accepted the belief that earrings warded off evil, seafarers from the time of the ancient Phoenicians relied on them as protection from the greatest evil they knew, being lost at sea.

EFFIGIES

Practitioners of Voodoo are said to be able to bring bad luck in the form of pain to their enemies by creating images of them that when cut or struck will affect the real person in the same way.

This method of transmitting bad luck is common in many cultures. The idea was commonly used in ancient India, Babylon and Egypt, and accounts of it are found in tribal histories in Africa and Australia. Native Americans were known to draw a figure of a person in sand or the ashes of a fire and poke it with a sharp stick to bring pain to an enemy. The Peruvian Indians made figures of fat mixed with grain, which they burned to destroy an enemy's soul. Bad luck was transmitted by the Malay tribes by collecting nail clippings and hair cuttings from an intended victim and incorporating them into a figure made from the wax of an abandoned bee's nest. This figure was slowly turned over the fire of a lamp for seven nights and on the last night, the victim would die.

In some cultures, these images are also intended to bring good fortune. In Sumatra, it is believed that if a barren woman holds a wooden figure of a child in her lap, she will be able to become pregnant. In some Pacific islands, a man who has fathered many children is asked to make a red cotton doll and present it to such a woman, who holds it to her breast to change her luck.

EGG

Our ancestors regarded the egg as a symbol of eternity, and the early Christians saw it as a sign of resurrection. In many cultures it is customary to give an egg to a new mother to bring good luck to her and to her child. In England, a gift of a white egg is considered generally lucky, but a brown egg, they say, will not only bring luck but happiness.

ELEPHANT

A bracelet made of elephant hair is said to bring luck to hunters and others who find fun in the great outdoors. Circus ringmasters traditionally sew a hair from an elephant's tail into the hem of their tailcoat to bring luck to the show. In India, amulets engraved with a representation of the god Ganesha, the elephant-headed Hindu god of wisdom, will bring the wearer foresight and will remove any and all obstacles from one's path. Charms in the form of elephant heads won't produce luck unless the trunk is in an upright position. Figures of elephants placed outside houses should always face the doorway to ensure they will bring luck to the household.

Elmo, Saint

In the days of sailing ships, a common phenomenon of lights on tall masts after a storm was known as Saint Elmo's fire. It is caused by static electricity, but sailors believed it to be a sign that Saint Elmo had brought them the luck that helped them survive the storm. The legend came from a time when Saint Elmo refused to stop preaching during a violent thunderstorm and survived when a lightning bolt struck him. The luck of Saint Elmo, still revered by all sailors, also extends to pregnant women, who can be protected from birth pains by the saint's intercession.

Emerald

The emerald has been considered an especially lucky stone for expectant mothers since ancient Egyptian women began wearing them. But its power to bring luck goes beyond that. In almost every part of the world, the green stone has been regarded for centuries as a special protector of eyesight. Indeed, the color itself is still regarded as best for protecting the eyes from glare, which is why accountants, editors, and others frequently wear green eyeshades. In some Far Eastern countries, emeralds are said to have the power to prevent loss of memory and dizziness. Some say the stone can help one uncover secrets and can give the gift of eloquence. Sailors and fishermen carry emeralds to protect them from storms at sea. In some cultures, lovers have been encouraged to wear emeralds to ensure constancy and openness between them. In ancient Persia, an emerald dangled from the right arm on a green cord was believed to protect travelers from highwaymen.

EVIL EYE

Just about every culture has believed in the power of the evil eye. According to the superstition, some people have the ability to call on evil spirits to have their wishes granted and bring harm, even death, to their enemies. The belief, the same the world over, stems from the concept that the eye is the source of all animal magnetism. It follows that the influence from the eyes of an envious or angry person can fill the air with an evil that affects not just living things, but inanimate objects as well. It could destroy a house, capsize a boat, cause crops to fail, or make a car roll into a ditch.

It is possible to counteract the evil, though, and ancient people began carrying amulets and charms to give them constant access to helpful good spirits. Many of them have come down to us as "lucky" charms, but their original intent was protection rather than luck.

The symbols most frequently used as shields against the evil eye are in the form of crescents and horns. Horns became the dominant symbol in Western cultures after the Greeks, and then the Romans, adapted the cow's head symbol of the Egyptian goddess Isis for their deities that protected crops and domestic cattle. Since the evil eye was believed capable of disrupting the food supply, it was only natural to turn to those gods and goddesses for protection against it.

Over time, the horns themselves became associated with divine protection. Today in Naples, where the evil eye is still perceived as very real, people invariably carry charms in the shape of horns to protect themselves. Their belief is so strong that if they feel threatened, it is considered enough just to say the word *corno!*—horn—and the threat will supposedly go away.

The protective power of animal horns is as much a worldwide phenomenon as the evil eye itself. Ceremonial masks from Cambodia are enhanced with them. So are wooden images of the gods of West Africa. Horned protectors have been found in Peru, in Tahiti, among the original inhabitants of North America, as well as in other parts of the world. Their purpose is the same everywhere: to counteract the evil eye.

FETISH

Similar to an amulet, a fetish is a natural object such as an animal tooth or bone, intended to create a bond between the human and supernatural worlds. The difference is that the fetish, common among animistic religions, is believed to be actually inhabited by spirits.

They are quite common in Africa where they are called *juju*, meaning "sacred object." French traders in West Africa translated the word to *joujou*, French for "plaything," which fostered the belief in Europe that these objects were toys. But they are taken very seriously by the cultures that use them.

Africans captured to be sold as slaves took their fetishes with them to the New World. Most were taken from them, however, because the slave traders regarded the fetishes as graven images, which offended their Christian sensibilities. The captives took to concealing their fetishes in small bags, which also contained herbs and oils they perceived as bringers of good luck. When they arrived in America, they made more of these collections of lucky charms, which came to be known as "gris-gris," or charm bags, a slang term for the *juju* of their ancestors.

Gris-gris, a staple of Voodoo, is usually a collection of bits of bone, colored stones, dust from a graveyard and salt and red pepper as well as other herbs. A red-flannel bag containing a magnet is a favorite lucky charm of gamblers. Although essentially intended to bring good luck, a charm bag is sometimes used to

bring bad luck to an enemy. It is frequently filled with gunpowder and red pepper and tossed into the enemy's path, a gesture
guaranteed to provoke a fight, often to the death. Such gris-gris
left at someone's door serves as a warning that bad luck will
follow unless fences are mended.

Fetishes were common among most Native American
tribes. The Zuni placed such great store in animals, birds and
snakes carved from shells or horns that they used them only in
religious ceremonies. They considered them far too powerful to
be left in the inexperienced hands of the common people.
Among other tribes, carvings representing mountain lions, eagles,
bears, coyotes and other animals were worn in leather pouches
around a hunter's neck to ensure luck in the hunt. To increase
the power of these objects, hunters often added bits of turquoise, colored stones and arrowheads to the pouch. Farmers'
fetishes usually contained seeds to ensure the continuation of
the cycle of life. Upon a man's death, the seeds were planted in
his fields. Fetishes that were not worn around the neck were
kept in sealed jars and ritually fed each day to strengthen their
power.

Indian fetishes carved from antlers were believed the most
powerful. Apart from the fact that they were made from living
tissue, such fetishes were associated with sea-serpents, the most
powerful of all animal gods.

FIRE

In the history of luck, few events can be considered as
important as the discovery of fire. Since that day, fire has been

worshiped by many cultures and is still among the most power-ful means of driving out evil, in spite of the fact that Satan is often personified as a being living in eternal fire.

Among the most common examples of building fires to bring luck, the bonfires kindled as part of religious ceremonies by Christians in the Middle Ages are still being lighted today in most parts of Europe. They occur in the spring and midsummer as well as in the fall and at Christmastime.

In Belgium and parts of Germany, such bonfires are kindled in the early days of Lent, when it is customary to burn seven of them simultaneously to protect the village from fire during the year ahead. In France, the Lenten fires are lighted by the last couple to be married in the district to bring luck to their union. While the fires are burning, farmers drive their livestock through the smoke to guard them against sickness. When the fire burns down to embers, young people leap across the red-hot coals to bring them luck in love, which they believe will be assured as long as their clothing is not singed. In Germany, the wood that will be consumed in the Lenten bonfire is arranged around a liv-ing beech tree in the form of a house or, as they call it, a castle. If the smoke blows in the direction of the cornfields, they believe they will have a lucky harvest.

In most of the Catholic countries of Europe, lights are extinguished on the night before Easter and a bonfire is built nearby. The parishioners pull burning sticks from them and carry them home, where they will be put into the hearth fire during summer thunderstorms to prevent lightning from striking. Sometimes, these charred sticks do double duty when they are kept in fields to protect the crops from hail. In Sweden, the building of the Easter fire is accompanied by gunfire, intended to drive evil spirits from the village.

In the Scottish Highlands, springtime bonfires were inherited from Druid rather than Christian influences, but the intent of bringing luck by fire is the same there as in other parts of Europe. The Scots believe that the fires of spring not only deter the influence of witches, but ensure good health for both man and beast. They also believe that the ashes from these fires have the power to neutralize any poison.

All over Europe, from the British Isles to the steppes of Russia, midsummer bonfires are built to drive away evil spirits. In nearly every case, it is believed that the height of the flames will match the height the corn or wheat will reach by harvesttime. In Scandinavia, these midsummer fires are believed to eliminate disease in cattle. The Scandinavians also believe that if they throw toadstools into the blaze, they will be protected from the influence of mischievous trolls. In Sweden, these fires are frequently kindled over wells, whose water will then acquire medicinal properties to heal the sick of the district. In Russia, the midsummer bonfires thwart witches bent on stealing milk from the local cows. On the morning after the fire, the boys who were responsible for building and tending it go from farm to farm collecting jugs of milk as their reward. They also attach burrs to fences around the cow pastures so that the animals will brush against them and in that way become immune to witches.

In France, any girl who dances around nine different midsummer bonfires will be lucky in love and will marry within the year. The French also march three times around these bonfires carrying branches of walnuts, which are taken home to be saved as a sure cure for toothaches.

In pagan cultures, midwinter fires were usually kindled indoors. Their legacy to Christendom is the Yule log. In Germany, this is a huge block of oak that is placed on the floor of the hearth, under the actual fire. Because the hearth fire is burned on top of it, the Yule log can last as long as a year, its glowing presence bringing luck to the household. In parts of Germany, the log is left in place only until it is thoroughly charred, after which it is removed and set aside to be returned to the fire during thunderstorms as a protection against lightning. In France, the Yule log is removed from the fire on Twelfth Night and placed under a bed to protect the house from catching fire. Its presence is also an antidote for chilblains. French farmers also scrape charred bits from the log and dissolve them in water, which is given to cows to help them at calving time. The ashes from the log are spread over the fields to prevent mildew in the crops. These same farmers also save some of the log's ashes to use in healing swollen glands, and when it has been reduced to a small lump of charcoal, the remains of the log are used as a wedge for their plows in the belief it has the power to make seeds sprout. French farm women shake pieces of the Yule log when it is removed on Twelfth Night. They believe that the number of sparks that fly from it will correspond to the number of chickens they will have in the coming year.

In England, the Yule log is lighted with a fragment of the previous year's log, which has been saved not only for this purpose, but to protect the house from fire and lightning. In Serbia, the log is usually oak, but often can be olive or birch. As it burns, they poke at it and the number of sparks produced predicts how many calves their herds will produce. When it has burned down, pieces of it are carried as a protection against hail.

Fish

Since the time the early Egyptians made figures of fish in gold and silver to bring luck to lovers, fish have been powerful luck producers. The Romans followed the Egyptian tradition that fish brought luck in courtship and marriage. In Japan, China, and other parts of the Far East, fish charms bring luck, wealth, and happiness. The early Christians adopted the fish as a symbol of courage and fidelity to God.

Fisherman's Luck

In New England, many professional fishermen insert a coin into a cork and set it afloat before leaving port in the morning. Their hope is that the offering will bring them luck in the form of a good catch. In other parts of America, fishermen who want their luck to continue make it a point to throw back the first fish they catch. In the South, where every fish counts, the first fish is hung from a tree instead. Some fishermen produce luck by spitting on the bait. Most believe that if someone asks them how many fish they've caught, revealing the number will prevent them from catching any more. Many also believe that changing poles during a day of fishing will result in bad luck.

FORTUNA

In the Broadway musical *Guys and Dolls*, one of the show-stopping numbers implores luck to be "a lady tonight." The idea of Lady Luck dates back to the ancient goddess known to the Romans as Fortuna, from whom we get our word "fortune." All riches, all bounty, all pleasure came directly from her, as did their opposites: poverty, need, unhappiness. Her power was more effective for women than for men. The earliest images of her show her with a wheel, symbolic of her ability to turn bad luck to good and vice versa (from which we have inherited our "wheel of fortune"), a globe symbolizing her worldwide influence, and a cornucopia for her ability to bring prosperity.

FOSSILS

Fossils are the only enduring evidence of plants and animals that fell into extinction long ago, being the impressions left in what has become rock and stone. Because of their age, history, and the fact that they were once alive, fossils unite the concepts of time, eternity, and evolution. For some, the continued existence of the impression of a once-living creature illustrates that the universe and the energy in it cannot be destroyed. In other words, matter can change forms to become something wholly different, but it can never be obliterated.

Generally, fossils are believed to increase an individual's innate defenses, and they are placed in the home and worn as jewelry to facilitate protection, but due to their age, they are often worn to increase longevity. Because of their connection to the past, fossils are often used to connect people with their past lives. They also confer to the bearer a sense of unity of time not possible without them. Amber and jet are two types of fossils that are said to advance a connection with the past and the eternity of earth.

FOUR-LEAF CLOVER

The four-leaf clover, possibly because it is relatively rare, has been a symbol of good luck for centuries. According to tradition, one leaf brings fame; one brings wealth; another insures good health; and the fourth, a faithful lover. But all clovers, even the ones with three leaves, have a special significance. Most of it is good, although the even rarer five-leaf clover was regarded as a symbol of death by the Druids of ancient Britain. Those same mysterious priests believed that carrying a four-leaf clover allowed them to see otherwise invisible witches and demons.

According to an older story, when Adam and Eve were expelled from Paradise, Eve took along a souvenir in the form of a four-leaf clover. It remained with her as a reminder of her happy days in the Garden of Eden. For generations of people, finding one in their own garden brought the same kind of happiness.

An old tradition says that a four-leaf clover stands for the arms of the cross, a powerful symbol even in pre-Christian times. It is also significant to many that the four leaves describe the points of the compass. Some cultures have believed that four-leaf clovers can prevent madness. Others say that if you find one you won't have to worry about being drafted into the military.

It is possible to buy four-leaf clovers encased in plastic. But true believers say that, like all lucky charms, the best luck comes from one you have found by chance.

President Abraham Lincoln carried a four-leaf clover most of his life. Whether his success as a lawyer and then as a politician can be credited to his lucky charm isn't known. But some say that one of the few times he did not have the clover in his pocket was when he went to the theater on April 14, 1865, when he was assassinated.

Frances of Rome, Saint

Frances was born in 1384 to a noble Roman family who promised her to Lorenzo Ponziano at age thirteen. Since the age of eleven, Frances had known that she wanted to be a nun, but she was a devoted wife nonetheless. She discovered that her sister-in-law, Vanozza, shared her love for the church, and together they ventured into Rome to care for the sick and poor. Eventually, Ponziano's family was forced from its lands by the invasion of Ladislas of Naples, but Frances and Vanozza continued their works.

During this time of exile and despair, Frances prayed and labored, and eventually she was given the gift of healing and a constant vision of her guardian angel. The light bestowed to her by this angel allowed her to see at night, which is the reason that today she is the saint invoked for safe motoring.

FROG

A charm or amulet in the shape of a frog is said to attract true friends and to help you find long-lasting love. Frogs are also said to be effective in speeding recovery from disease. Among the ancient Egyptians and Greeks, frogs symbolized inspiration and fertility, and the Romans believed that frogs brought good luck to a household. In the fashion world, an ornamental loop and fastener on a coat is called a frog because its original design was adapted from frogs embroidered on clothes for good luck.

GARLIC

As most moviegoers know, the best protection against vampires is a necklace of garlic. But apart from that, garlic has long been considered an effective lucky charm for curing illness, as well as for relief from toothaches and for preventing colds.

Roman soldiers carried garlic to give them courage. Some farmers believe that if a horse is ailing, rubbing its teeth with garlic will restore its health by making it eat, well, like a horse.

GARNET

This wine-red stone is a charm that ensures constancy and is often given as a gift between friends who are parted. It is also sometimes used in engagement rings. In ancient Persia, garnets were worn to avoid being struck by lightning, and the Persians also believed that the stone could prevent fevers. Given as a gift, a garnet will bring happiness, but if one is stolen, the thief will experience nothing but bad luck.

GENEVIÈVE, SAINT

Geneviève became a nun at the prodding of Saint Germanus of Auxerre during her childhood in France, at the age of fifteen. She lived during a time of great turbulence for France, especially since during her lifetime in A.D. 451, Attila the Hun threatened Paris. During his advance on the city, Geneviève told the residents to stay indoors and pray vigorously. Eventually Attila the Hun left and moved on to Orléans, sparing Paris. Since this was the first disaster averted by the heartfelt prayers of Geneviève, she is viewed as a prime protector from disasters.

When the Franks were threatening Paris after the impending danger from Attila the Hun was dispelled, she led a group up the River Seine to retrieve corn and supplies so that the Parisians would not starve. She persuaded the Frankish king, Childeric, to release French prisoners, gaining the respect of both the king and his son Clovis, who would later convert to Christianity and found the church of Saint Peter and Paul, which later became the church of Sainte-Geneviève. For her divine sanctity and overwhelming success in averting crises and dangers, she is today revered and invoked against disaster of all kinds.

GLOVES

A gift of a pair of gloves will strengthen a friendship, according to a very old belief. The gloves themselves become a good-luck charm, bringing happiness to the one who receives them. In the Victorian era, women were usually not permitted to accept any gift from a man except for gloves or flowers, and a bet made between a man and a woman was usually paid with a pair of gloves.

Goldfish

As well as being one of the sacred emblems of Buddha, the goldfish, a member of the carp family, either in the flesh or as a good-luck charm, is revered all over the Orient. It brings luck in the form of long life. The ancient Egyptians believed that having goldfish in the house was especially lucky for the whole family. The Greeks thought they brought good luck to a marriage.

Grateful Dead

More than the name of a rock group, the term "grateful dead" refers to ghosts of the departed who return to bring good luck to the living. In most traditions, this is based on the concept of returning a favor. In the Middle Ages, it was common to bury the impoverished dead in mass graves. If someone volunteered to pay for a proper burial, that person would eventually meet a stranger who would bring good fortune. Stories told of such encounters always include a demand of half the proceeds of the windfall, which, if agreed upon, results in the revelation that the luck has come directly from a spirit of the dead.

In China, where proper burial is the only way the dead can be honored in the tradition of ancestor worship, the kindness of strangers is rewarded with the greatest of good fortune by the grateful dead.

GREMLINS

After Charles Lindbergh made the first solo flight from New York to Paris in 1927, he became known all over the world as "Lucky Lindy." But, as he revealed in his autobiography more than twenty-five years later, he wasn't really all alone on that flight. His luck might have come from the influence of spirits that are now called gremlins.

According to Lindbergh's account, by the ninth hour of his thirty-three hour flight, he became fatigued and disoriented. It was then he began to notice that the cockpit was filled with vague shapes that, though in the form of cloud-like vapor, had the power of speech. They were quite friendly, said Lindbergh, and they reassured him that he'd eventually land safely in Paris. They also offered him help with the navigation.

These creatures were first reported by British pilots in World War I, who gave them the name of gremlins (a term inspired by Grimm's fairy tales), but generally kept silent about them. Although the gremlins were friendly and helpful, it has long been considered bad luck to speak openly of even helpful spirits and the pilots didn't want to push their luck.

The little creatures made a reappearance in 1939, when they allegedly sabotaged a British bomber in the early stages of World War II. They have since been spotted, or their influence felt, repeatedly by crews of both military and commercial aircraft.

As the 1939 episode suggests, gremlins are as capable of bringing bad luck as good. Among reported incidents, they seem to have a fondness for drinking aviation fuel and love to chew through electrical lines. But although mischievous, they are perceived as being generally friendly. They have an uncommon knowledge of meteorology and aerodynamics, and scores of pilots swear they were able to bring badly damaged planes to safe landings with the help of gremlins on board.

Although there have been thousands of gremlin sightings over the years, few airmen seem able to agree about what one looks like. To Lindbergh, they were as formless as puffs of smoke. Some World War II pilots described them as little human-like creatures about six inches tall with horns on their heads. Others claim they look more like wild rabbits or terriers. One fighter pilot, who believes he owes his life to a gremlin, swears his benefactor had webbed feet and fins like a fish.

Hands

In just about every Mediterranean country, charms in the shape of human hands have been powerful symbols of good luck. In Muslim countries, the hand is made with the thumb and fingers outstretched in honor of Fatima, the favorite daughter of the prophet Mohammed. Fatima was one of only three women worthy of entering heaven. The thumb represents the prophet himself, the first finger represents Fatima, the middle finger her husband, and the others her two sons. The ancient Etruscans and the Greeks wore lucky amulets representing a fist with the thumb tucked beneath the fingers. Similar charms with the index finger extended were believed to have power to ward off the evil eye.

Sometimes a simple hand gesture encourages good luck or helps ward off bad luck. In most Christian churches, worshipers are blessed with the age-old sign of the benediction, with the minister's first and second fingers outstretched and the thumb and other fingers closed over the palm. In many countries, but especially in Italy, the evil eye is thwarted with the so-called "devil's horn," the fist clenched with the index and little fingers outstretched.

HEART

Charms in the shape of hearts are obviously intended to bring luck in love. Among the ancient Egyptians, such charms were also believed to have power over the influences of black magic.

HEX SIGN

One of the delights of a visit to the Amish areas of Pennsylvania, Ohio, and Indiana is the huge round designs painted on the sides of the barns. Ask a farmer what they mean and he'll probably tell you they are "chust for pretty." But don't believe it. They are hex signs and they are there to protect the barn and the livestock inside from the influence of witches. The designs are usually circles within circles, following the belief that devils, witches, and other evil beings can't cross into a circle or, more important, out of one.

Although hex signs are painted in many bright colors, the predominant one is red, known to frighten the devil and all his kind. The name for them, "hex," refers to the witch's own weapon, the ability to cast a spell, or hex. The hex sign is intended to cast the spell on the witch before she can put one on the barn.

HOLLY

Although it is one of the most enduring symbols of Christmas, holly was the gift of good luck among the Romans celebrating their midwinter festivals. The northern tribes, who eventually brought about Rome's downfall, draped holly over doorways as shelter for friendly woodland spirits who could bring good luck to their houses. In medieval Europe, it was planted under windows because people believed it repelled witches.

Sprigs of holly in the house at Christmastime will bring you good luck. But be careful not to bring it indoors before Christmas Eve or your family will fall to squabbling. (Bet you were wondering why that happens—blame it on the holly brought indoors too soon.) And be sure to burn it on Twelfth Night (January 5) or the good luck will turn sour.

HOMOBONUS, SAINT

Homobonus, a name that means "good man," was aptly given to this merchant of Cremona in Italy. He believed that his business was an employment given to him by God, which led him to conduct his business dealings with high morality and honesty. He also donated a large portion of the proceeds from his business to the poor, which is why he is known as the patron saint of businesspeople.

HORN

Like crescents, which they resemble, charms in the form of animal horns are believed to have great power over the evil eye. Because of that special power, horns rank among the most effective bringers of good luck. The belief in the power of the horn extends to cultures all over the world and is among the most ancient in the world of luck.

HORSE

Probably because of their key role in advancing civilizations, horses have been regarded as lucky in nearly every civilization the world has ever known. Charms and amulets in the shape of a horse, or a horse's head, are able to help the wearer rise to new heights of achievement and happiness. In eastern Europe today, it is still believed that a face-to-face encounter with a pinto horse will make a wish come true. But those same people also believe that making eye contact with an all-white horse will bring bad luck unless they quickly spit three times over their left shoulder.

Horseshoe

If you hang a horseshoe over your door, be careful to hang it with the points upward. Even little children know this prevents the luck from running out. But here's an older explanation from the Middle Ages: Bad luck can become trapped within the circle formed by the horseshoe. Because the devil can't cross the opening, he will be doomed to run back and forth inside.

According to folk wisdom, the reason the devil can't cross the opening of a horseshoe when he is perfectly capable of flying through an open window is that Satan and all his minions are terrified of iron. The crescent shape of a horseshoe makes it even more lucky.

The Greeks and Romans nailed horseshoes to their walls to protect them from plagues. In the Middle Ages, horseshoes were often buried in the roots of an ash tree, which was considered among the luckiest of trees. It was believed that the branches of an ash growing around a horseshoe needed only to be waved over the backs of cattle to instantly cure them of any ill.

Although horseshoes are most often hung over doorways, fishermen along England's east coast nail them to the masts of their boats to ensure lucky catches. And one of the most successful sailors of them all, Admiral Lord Nelson, had a horseshoe nailed to the mast of his flagship, H.M.S. Victory, when he took on the Spanish and French fleets at the Battle of Trafalgar. Whether it did any good is open to question. Lord Nelson was killed in the battle, but his fleet was victorious and his ship—and the British Empire—were saved.

HOT CROSS BUN

Hot cross buns, although usually associated with Lent and Easter, actually predate Christianity by centuries. Among ancient cultures that worshiped the moon, the buns, which were eaten during religious festivals, represented the full moon, and the cross represented its four quarters. To these early believers, hot cross buns were symbols of good fortune. They still are. People believe they are very effective charms against the powers of the devil. Some say that putting one under a baby's pillow will help the child sleep quietly through the night. They are also quite popular among sailors and fishermen, who feel that keeping a hot cross bun aboard ship will protect the vessel from shipwreck.

HUNCHBACK

Among many primitive peoples, those among them with physical deformities are frequently regarded as lucky. One of those beliefs that has found its way into the civilized world is that hunchbacked people have the power to changes one's luck for the better. It was a prevalent belief among the ancient Egyptians and the Persians. In modern times, the idea is especially strong among gamblers, who find it effective to stroke a hunchback's hump before picking a card or rolling dice.

Obviously, it isn't always possible to have a real hunchback handy to change one's luck. In Italy, the problem has been solved by making little figurines of humans with humps on their back, which are believed to be an effective substitute for the real thing. These little images are called "Gobbos," after the character

Lancelot Gobbo in Shakespeare's *The Merchant of Venice*. Unlike traditional lucky charms that are made of materials occurring in nature, most Gobbos are made of plastic. They invariably have leering faces with bulging eyes and are dressed in tuxedos and top hats. Good luck is believed to follow the rubbing of the protrusion on the Gobbo's back.

IDES OF MARCH

Shakespeare tells us that Julius Caesar was warned to "Beware the Ides of March." It is a historical fact that Caesar was assassinated on that day, roughly March 15, in 44 B.C. But to the average Roman, it was considered a rather lucky day. On that day it was customary for the Plebs, the common people, to take the day off for picnics along the River Tiber. Drinking wine was part of the celebration, and it was believed that luck was ensured by it. Every cup of wine a person consumed represented a year added to his or her life.

JADE

Serious gamblers, especially those who play the horses, consider jade to be a lucky stone. Although astrologers claim that the brilliant green mineral can bring bad luck to people born under the signs of Sagittarius or Gemini, beads and amulets made from it are regarded as lucky charms all over the world.

From earliest times in China, jade charms in the shape of bats or storks have been believed to ensure long life. Jade carvings worn around the neck have been powerful lucky charms among the Chinese since the fourteenth century B.C. Even today, a Chinese businessperson might feel luckier holding a jade amulet when making important decisions.

In other parts of the world, jade is regarded as a charm against problems with the eyes. And from ancient times through the Middle Ages, it was used as a prescription for curing kidney and digestive diseases. When Europeans first arrived in Central America, they were amazed to discover that the Incas in Peru shared this belief and routinely relied on jade charms to prevent kidney problems.

In many cultures, jade amulets are considered the best possible protection for women in childbirth. Some believe the stone is a bringer of rain and that it can drive away wild beasts and evil spirits. It is said to cure dropsy, abolish thirst and relieve palpitations of the heart. Few charms are more effective in assuring victory in battle or protecting against being struck by lightning.

JASPER

Jasper is a stone of various luck-bringing powers. It confers the powers of health, security, and beauty to its wearers. It is called the "rain-bringer" because of the success Native Americans had in conjuring rain from the sky with the help of jasper. Most commonly, jasper is worn to increase mental processes and to subdue any unruly desires or wishes that may cause harm to the bearer. However, each color of jasper has its own powers and brings its own form of luck.

Ancient peoples engraved red jasper with images of archers and lions and carried the carvings to ward off poisons and to alleviate fevers. It also can have a "mirror" effect, such that it reflects evil back to the originator. Healing, beautification, and gracefulness are also attributed to red jasper.

Green jasper is effective in preventing illness, especially when placed in a circle around a green candle. This same technique aids in encouraging the body toward a more restorative sleep pattern. In another vein, green jasper aids in the bearer's understanding of others' emotional states.

If you plan on going swimming sometime soon, you may want to carry a piece of mottled jasper with you, as its main power is to protect its wearer from drowning. Also, if you have difficulty concentrating on the real world and happen to daydream often, wear a brown jasper to bring you and your thoughts back to earth.

JEROME, SAINT

Born in A.D. 341 in Dalmatia, Jerome is considered the patron saint of students. He became a priest rather reluctantly since he believed his true calling lay in the monastic life. His passion was the classic works of literature and he devoted many scholarly hours to their study.

In Rome under Saint Damascus, he was commissioned to write a standard Latin text of the Bible, today called the Vulgate. He was occupied in the writing of this version for the next twenty-two years, and the intense level of scholarship and study necessary to complete such a task is the reason that he is the patron saint of students.

JUDE, SAINT

Anyone who feels dogged by a run of bad luck can turn to Saint Jude for help. Well known as the patron saint of hopeless causes, newspapers the world over carry personal columns filled with petitions to Saint Jude and expressions of gratitude for his help in turning bad luck to good. Although one of the original disciples appointed by Jesus, his name was often confused with that of Judas, the betrayer. Because of this, early Christians praying to the saints avoided seeking help from Jude out of fear of confusion. He became the saint of last resort, resorted to by the desperate only after prayers to other saints had failed.

KACHINA

The Pueblo, Hopi and Zuni nations of the American Southwest place great store in the luck-bringing properties of these dolls. They represent native spirits and each is dressed in elaborate costume. Although regularly used in tribal ceremonies, these dolls, known as kachinas, are also used as playthings by children and displayed in homes as well as in sacred places. It is believed that by making the spirit represented by the doll an intimate member of the family group, luck will come to that family in the form of good harvests and protection from natural disasters.

KEY

A key given as a gift between lovers is considered a symbol of unlocking the door to the heart. It is believed that the giver will be lucky in love. As a symbol of luck, a single key is among the most important, not to mention one of the oldest, of charms. The Greeks and Romans believed it represented the Key of Life and had the power to unlock the door through which prayers reached the gods. They attached special significance to keys made of silver, the metal sacred to the goddess Diana. She was the protector of doorways and thresholds as well as the special guardian of mothers-to-be. As the Key of Life, it was worn as a talisman to promote remembrance of things past and foresight for things to come.

Among the Japanese, three keys tied together are considered a powerful lucky charm. They enable the wearer to unlock the doors that lead to love, health, and wealth. According to the Gypsies of eastern Europe, a door key with a metal ring attached will ensure a good night's sleep if it is hung upside down over the bed. It will also prevent nightmares.

Knocking on Wood

In some places it's called "touching wood," but knocking on wood for luck is an almost universal compulsion. The idea probably dates back to prehistoric times, when people believed that the gods lived inside trees. Touching a tree was a way of acknowledging the deity and of securing its favor.

It all began with the idea that the air around us is filled with demons whose sole purpose is to cancel out good fortune. The best way to prevent that is to be careful not to talk about good things that come your way. But if the words should slip out, the next best thing is to knock on wood to get the attention of the good spirits. They will use their power to help you keep your good luck. It helps if you knock three times. Evil spirits can't cope with the power of the number three.

Knot

In many cultures, a knot tied in a piece of string, a rope or an article of clothing is perceived as an instrument of bad luck. In the Middle Ages, when a woman went into labor, all knots of any kind in the house were quickly untied and all locks, on doors, cupboards and chests were opened. In parts of India, this custom is still followed throughout the entire pregnancy. In the Pacific islands, it is taboo for either the man or the woman to tie knots of any kind or even to cross their legs during the entire term of a pregnancy.

All these customs relate to a belief that knots will "tie up" the woman and bring her the bad luck of a difficult delivery. In

China, where the same belief is prevalent, difficult births are eased not only by opening doors and windows and cutting knots, but by removing stoppers from bottles and bungs from barrels. At the same time all the animals on a farm are turned loose—cows are untied in their stalls, horses are sent out to pasture and even the family dog is unleashed.

In West Africa, when a woman is giving birth, the medicine man ties her feet and hands together and then ceremoniously cuts the knots. The vines he has used as cords are then cut into pieces and boiled in water that is used to bathe the woman to ease her pain.

The idea that crossing one's legs could bring bad luck to a pregnant woman was also apparently strong among the ancient Romans. Pliny, the Roman naturalist, wrote that to sit beside a pregnant woman, or anyone undergoing any kind of medical treatment, with clasped hands would result in the casting of an evil spell over that person. Pliny also wrote that the spell would be more intense if one were to rub their leg with clasped hands or "lay one leg over the other." He reported that the same evil influence would follow if these acts were performed at business meetings or during sacrifices or prayers.

In the Middle Ages, it was believed that one could prevent the consummation of a marriage by tying a knot in a cord while the ceremony was taking place. To do its malevolent work, the knotted cord was thrown into flowing water. Marital bliss could not follow until the cord was found and the knot untied. In parts of Africa today, the same bad luck can be visited upon a marriage if the bridegroom has buttoned any of the buttons on his wedding suit, and an enemy can bring him bad luck by tying a knot in a handkerchief and slipping it into his pocket.

The Koran mentions the evil influence of "those who puff into the knots." This refers to an incident in which an enemy of Mohammed tied nine knots in a string and dropped it into a well to bring mischief to the prophet. The trick might have worked, but the angel Gabriel revealed what had happened, the knotted string was retrieved, and Mohammed was able to force each of the knots to untie itself by reciting charms over them.

There are occasions, however, when knots can bring good luck. The Romans believed it was possible to cure ailments of the groin by tying seven knots in a spider's web and applying it to the afflicted area. In Arabia, seven knots tied in thread made from camel's hair and fashioned into a bracelet are believed to have the power to cure illnesses. One knot is untied each day as the bracelet is blown upon. When the seventh knot is untied, the thread is rolled into a ball and thrown into running water, which carries the ailment away with it.

In Russia, knots are considered effective to drive away the influence of evil magicians. A fishing net, which contains hundreds of knots, is always thrown over a bride on her wedding day. The bridegroom and the male attendants wear belts made of fishing nets to bring them luck during the ceremony. Russian peasants routinely carry amulets that are simply bits of yarn with knots tied in them. Such protectors made of red wool are often wrapped around children's legs and arms to prevent colds; and one wrapped nine times around a child's neck is believed to have the power to prevent scarlet fever.

LADDER

Even people who don't believe in luck usually make it a point to avoid walking under a ladder. It's probably a good idea because you never know if someone up there might drop something on you. Ladders have been considered lucky symbols for centuries. The Egyptians usually placed them in their tombs to help the souls of the dead climb heavenward. They also carried charms in the form of ladders, to help avoid earthly temptation and to climb to greater heights. Ladders also appear along with other symbols of good luck on talismans that were carried in all parts of the world well into the Middle Ages.

Ladders enter the realm of the unlucky when they are leaned against a wall to form a triangle with the ground. The same triangle is formed by an open stepladder. The three sides are believed to represent the basic family unit—father, mother, and child, and passing through it can violate the unity of the family. Others say the triangle represents the Trinity—Father, Son, and Holy Spirit, the unity of which must also never be interrupted.

There is an antidote, of course. If you should unwittingly wander under a ladder, you can save yourself by crossing your fingers and spitting three times through the ladder's rungs.

LADYBUG

"Ladybug, ladybug, fly away home." You've probably said that yourself when one of these little red beetles landed on your sleeve. But in spite of the command, it's considered very good luck to be visited by a ladybug. If a ladybug lands on you, money will come your way. Kill her and the money you already have will fly away.

LAPIS LAZULI

Lapis lazuli is a protective stone that has overwhelming powers for conferring good luck and good humor to the wearer. Its most basic powers include the ability to encourage love and affection, and to dissipate depression, thereby infusing the wearer with peaceful bliss.

Lapis lazuli contains a combination of many powers. It can be essential in creating peace and a sense of well-being as well as wisdom and sanctity. Its other powers include healing, loyalty, bravery, and protection.

Lapis lazuli has strong connections to royalty, some of which date back to ancient Sumer. The Sumerians believed that if one were to carry the stone close to the body, the powers of the deities would be conferred to the carrier. Today, the stone is often found to be extremely uplifting to downtrodden spirits brought on by a string of bad luck. The blue color of the stone signifies the soothing qualities and powers it gives to the bearer. Most important, it is effective in alleviating depression, as well as attracting spiritual love.

Some people have used lapis lazuli with success in their search for spiritual love. First, find a piece of lapis lazuli with a sharp edge and warm the tip in the flame of a pink candle while thinking of your need for love. Then carve a heart into the candle with the sharp edge of the lapis lazuli, placing the stone beside the candlestick upon completion. Continue to burn the candle and visualize a heightened spiritual love entering your life. For a simpler path to good luck in love, wear a charm made of lapis lazuli to cement the connection formed between romantic partners.

Lizard

If your heart skips a beat when a lizard slithers past, you are not alone. But the ancients considered them to be very handy to have around. Our ancestors, who often slept under the stars, believed that if a lizard appeared, it was bringing a warning that a poisonous snake was lurking nearby. Lucky charms in the shape of lizards are said to have the power to preserve the eyesight of the wearer. Some people believe that anyone who kills a lizard will pay for the act with failing vision. The creature is also often regarded as a protector of unborn children. If an expectant mother wears a lizard charm, she will be more likely to give birth to a happy, healthy baby. Even better, if a live lizard crosses her path, her child will have a long and prosperous life.

LODESTONE

Amulets and talismans made from magnetite, a form of iron oxide, have been considered lucky for centuries because of their mysterious magnetic powers. In fact, these luck-producers, known as lodestones, were considered so powerful the ancients decreed they could only take the form of a necklace or be set in a ring.

Placed on a bed, a lodestone is regarded as an irresistible aphrodisiac that calls any woman immediately to love. But at the same time, if the stone is set in a ring of pure silver, it is believed to inspire chastity.

It has long been believed that if a man soaks a lodestone in oil and then anoints himself with it, his virility will be enhanced. And as a pleasant side effect, the oil will also impart vigor and robust health. This same effect can be obtained by eating from plates made of magnetite, a little tricky if one uses metal knives and forks, which will be attracted to the plate.

Among ancient beliefs regarding magnetite is that it has the power to attract pain into itself, which makes it valuable in the treatment of every ailment imaginable. Placed on a woman's thigh, a lodestone is said to ease the pains of childbirth.

Soldiers with a conscience believe that a weapon that has been rubbed against a lodestone creates wounds that are both painless and bloodless.

LUCKS

Until recent times in England, many aristocratic families collected ornate dishes, cups and glassware that were handed down from generation to generation as symbols of good luck and protection against evil influences. It was believed that these special heirlooms, known as "lucks," would keep the family prosperous as long as they were not broken.

Tradition dictated that lucks could not be purchased but must be gifts. It was customary for royalty to give such gifts, but many families claim that their lucks were presented to them by fairies or some other magical creature.

One of the most famous of these items is the Luck of Edenhall, a thick brown glass decorated in red, blue and gold. It is kept in a special leather case in a castle in northern England. According to its official history, it came into the possession of the Musgrave family in the fifteenth century when a butler went to the well to fetch water and interrupted a group of fairies at play. When they saw him coming, they scattered but left their cup behind. As they hurried away, one called back, "If this cup should ever break or fall, farewell the Luck of Edinhall." It became famous three hundred years later when a drunken guest let it slip through his fingers and it was caught in the nick of time by an alert servant.

Another, whose powers may be questionable, is the Luck of Muncaster, a green glass cup with gold and white decorations. It was said to have been given to the owner of Muncaster Castle by King Henry VI in 1464. The king had been forced from his throne during the Wars of the Roses and while wandering through the countryside, he was refused shelter everywhere he went. When Sir John Pennington welcomed him to Muncaster, Henry rewarded him with the cup and said that as long as it was preserved unbroken, the Pennington family would never be without a male heir. The prediction seemed to work for more than three hundred years, but in the eighteenth century, the family name died due to a lack of male Penningtons. The cup was still unbroken.

The powers attributed to lucks were forgotten after the industrial revolution when many of the English gentry found it necessary to sell off family heirlooms to maintain their lifestyles. Some might believe that by selling their lucks, these families doomed themselves to continuing bad luck.

LUCKY CLOTHING

Millions of people have an article of clothing that they believe will bring them luck when they are wearing it. Athletes are famous for their lucky shirts, actors are well-known for items from handkerchiefs to neckties to specific shoe styles they believe will ensure a good performance and students frequently choose something special to wear when they show up for that big test. It is a rare bride who does not walk down the aisle wearing "something old, something new, something borrowed, something blue" for luck in her coming marriage. Many also place a coin in their shoe as a good-luck bonus.

But in the days of the Mogul emperors in India, before the British came in the eighteenth century, lucky clothing was almost never actually worn. This clothing was a gift from the emperor himself, bestowed in a ceremony known as the *durbar*. It involved the ceremonial exchange of gifts, coins for the emperor and cloaks and turbans to his honored guests. These items of clothing brought prestige to people who received them and were symbols of the greatest good luck. They were displayed in the recipient's home and always became family heirlooms, handed down from generation to generation, a gift of luck from one's ancestors.

A tradition in China is to have the clothes one will be buried in made during their lifetime, even though they will not wear them until they are dead. It is common to have these grave clothes made by an unmarried woman in the belief that she has a long life ahead of her and this will be transferred to her work. It is considered best to have the clothes made during a leap year, whose length implies that life will also be long. Among these costumes, the one considered luckiest is known as a longevity garment. It is a deep-blue silk robe with the word longevity embroidered on it in gold thread. Unlike other burial clothes, the longevity garment is proudly worn at important festivals, when it believed the power of the golden letters will be enhanced. It is especially important, if one hopes for a long life, to wear the robe during birthday celebrations. It is believed that on these occasions the person will absorb health and vigor that will last through the coming year. Longevity garments are quite expensive and are commonly obtained as gifts from one's children late in life.

In ancient Greece, people initiated into the super-secret religious cult, the Eleusinian Mysteries, gave the costumes they wore during the induction ceremonies to mothers, who cut them up to make clothes for their babies. Everyone believed that these clothes had the power to bring good luck and long life to infants who wore them.

Among the Plains Indians, especially the Sioux, in the late nineteenth century, a cult known as Ghost Dancers emerged with the promise that its followers would prevent the white man from taking over their traditional hunting grounds. Their magic was said to come from elaborate dances they performed, but the edge of luck came from the shirts they wore. Anyone wearing one, it was believed, was protected from bullets, spears or any other instruments of death.

At the same time, half a world away, a Chinese cult known as the Fists of Righteous Harmony, commonly called the Boxers, believed a similar lucky shirt brought the same sort of protection. The Boxers extended the protection to death by drowning as well as from guns and cannons.

MALACHITE

Luck in business will follow you if you discover the powers of malachite. It is the salesperson's stone and it is believed to bring power, protection, love, and tranquility. Traditionally, people wore malachite to ward off and discover oncoming peril. When danger is near at hand, malachite spontaneously breaks into pieces to warn the wearer of the potential difficulty ahead.

In business, malachite, like bloodstone, will bring good luck and success if placed in a cash register. Similarly, if pieces of malachite are placed in each corner of an office building, customers will be drawn to the establishment. If success at conventions or business meetings is desired, malachite should be worn in order to increase the probability of gaining good deals.

In order to protect against impending dangers, wear malachite pendants or beads. If you are searching for love, or hoping to increase a love you have already found, try wearing a malachite necklace that touches the skin near the heart, since it is widely believed that this will increase your capacity to love and the ability of love to find you.

If you are currently having difficulty sleeping, try wearing a malachite necklace to bed since it is said to increase your sense of peacefulness and reinforce sleep. Also, holding malachite in your hand and looking at it promotes calmness and the overall relaxation of the nervous system, and it also removes feelings of depression.

MASCOT

When football players take time out, fans usually turn their attention to the team's mascot. Sometimes it can be a real animal, like the mule that goes to all the Army games. Or it can be a mythical creature, like the leprechaun that brings the "luck o' the Irish" to Notre Dame. But those symbols—whether a man dressed up like a chicken, or a goat at the end of a leash—are there for much more than your entertainment. They are lucky charms.

The word *mascot* at one time applied to all charms, amulets, and talismans. Its modern meaning is an animal, a person, or an object adopted by a group to bring it luck. Jupiter, the most powerful of the Roman gods, was said to have an eagle as his mascot, and the Roman legions adopted the bird as their lucky symbol. The same mascot worked well for Napoleon's army, too. And its eagle mascot has brought a good deal of good luck to the United States of America.

MAY DAY

The ancients believed in the luck-bringing qualities of many trees which they perceived as the dwelling places of the gods. By the Middle Ages, tree-worship had been largely forgotten, but people continued to believe that trees and tree branches could bring them luck. On the first of May, it became customary for young people to cut down a sycamore tree and carry it into the village, where its trunk would be erected in the square. The branches were cut from it and placed over doorways to bring luck to the household during the season of planting.

The tradition is still prevalent in most parts of Europe. In parts of France, a girl designated "Little May Rose" for the day accompanies other children from house to house collecting gifts. Ignoring her is believed to bring bad luck to anyone who isn't forthcoming with a coin or some offering of food. Boys in the same area roam the countryside on the same day begging for gifts from farm families. If they are satisfied with what they get, they plant a tree in front of the house, a gesture that will bring luck to the farmer in the form of a good crop.

Médard, Saint

Saint Médard is believed to be helpful in holding off bad weather. He is also frequently invoked against toothaches. He was ordained a priest at age thirty, but was sixty when he became bishop of Vermand, his position until his death. Saint Médard performed numerous acts of charity and kindness. For one of those acts, an eagle rewarded him by sheltering him from a thunderstorm with its wings. He is therefore shown in most medieval paintings with an eagle hovering above his head, sheltering him from the storm, which is the reason he is principally invoked against bad weather and tempests of all kinds.

Mezuzah

A small tube with a piece of parchment inside is frequently fastened to the doorways of Jewish homes to bring God's blessing to the household. The parchment is inscribed with the words "Hear, O Israel: The Lord our God is one Lord." The passage is from the Book of Deuteronomy, in which Moses not only commands his people to keep these words in their hearts, but to "write them upon the posts of thy house, and on thy gates." For added luck, people passing through the doorway touch the mezuzah as a way of noting God's presence. The practice of protecting doorways with inscriptions is also common among Muslims, who carve verses from the Koran on them.

MIRROR

Break a mirror, they say, and seven years' bad luck will follow. Actually, it isn't the mirror that brings trouble, it's the image it reflects. The superstition has existed for centuries—long before glass mirrors were developed. It exists today among aboriginal people who have never seen a mirror.

Since prehistoric times, it was a common belief that to see one's own face was to see the life force, the soul itself. The usual way to see such a reflection was in a pool of water, and if an enemy should toss a stone into it and break the reflection, evil was sure to follow. Many also believed that if the reflection was taken completely away, the soul would go away, too. Death would result.

As mirrors became more common and mankind more enlightened, the belief that the face reflects the soul faded away. But there was always that nagging fear that breaking a looking glass could be unlucky. For hundreds of years it was believed that the cells that make up one's body are completely renewed every seven years. That meant, obviously, that if you are cursed with bad luck when your reflection is destroyed, it can't last forever. You'll be a whole new person in seven years. When that happens, your luck will change for the better. Unless, of course, you've broken another mirror in the meantime.

MISTLETOE

Stand under a sprig of mistletoe and you're sure to get kissed. If that in itself isn't a sign of good luck, consider its deeper meaning. According to a Viking legend, after Baldur, the son of the goddess Friga, died and was restored to life, her tears of gratitude turned into the white berries of the mistletoe. A sprig of mistletoe used as a dart is what killed Baldur in the first place, and when he was resurrected, his mother proclaimed that the plant was now sacred to her and would never again be used for evil purposes. Friga was the Norse goddess of love, and from that moment to this, anyone kissed under mistletoe falls under her special protection.

MOONSTONE

The milky white stone with a hint of blue gets its name from its resemblance to soft moonlight. In India, where they are common and considered bringers of good luck, the moonstones with the greatest power are those washed up with the tide when the moon and sun are aligned. The stone is used in other parts of the world as a lucky charm to bring parted lovers together again. It is also believed to have the power to cure some diseases, including kidney problems, and to protect travelers. In medieval Europe, moonstones were regarded as indispensable when making important decisions. People who wished to be guided on the right path waited until the moon began to wane, and then placed a moonstone in their mouth. Then, by concentrating hard on the problem while sucking on the moonstone, the solution would come before the night was through.

New Year

In China, where the New Year arrives with the first full moon after the sun enters Aquarius (January 20, according to our calendar), it is time to give gifts of money or gold to bring good luck during the coming year.

Almost every culture has special beliefs reserved for the first day of the year, all of them intended to make a new beginning and to ensure good luck. In some places, it is customary to open the windows at midnight on New Year's Eve so good luck will fly in and bad luck will fly out. It is also considered important nearly everywhere to make as much noise as possible with noisemakers and horns, church bells, and fireworks to encourage the bad luck to go away. If someone kisses you on New Year's Eve, you'll be kissed frequently all year long. And if you take a drink at the stroke of midnight, you'll have good luck. It will be even better if you drink the last of the contents of the bottle— but be careful. You won't feel so lucky the next day if you have to drink the first half of the bottle to get to the bottom half!

Numbers

Every number has a special significance and according to ancient astrologers and numerologists, every person has a lucky number. In general, odd numbers are considered luckier than even ones.

Our ancestors who developed the idea of lucky numbers didn't all agree on how to arrive at one, though. Some said that you should add up only the vowels in your first name. Others said the consonants held the key. And still others were convinced that you should add up all the letters of your name plus your birthday. Nearly all numerologists agree with the rule set down by the Greek mathematician Pythagoras in the sixth century. There are only nine numbers, he said. All the rest are simply multiples and therefore repetitious.

One simple way of finding your own lucky number is by adding:

1. The day of the month you were born
2. The number of the month
3. The number of the year

The sum of those numbers added together is a widely accepted key to your lucky number. For example, someone born on November 7, 1945, the seventh day of the eleventh month, would add 7+11+1945. Then the result, 1,963, is added again: 1+9+6+3 to arrive at the number 19. Add 1+9, which equals 10. Then reduce this number to a single digit by adding the two numbers: 1+0=1. One is the lucky number.

But apart from giving you a start on the sequence to use next time you buy a lottery ticket, it will be helpful to understand the significance of numbers.

ONE

As a symbol of beginnings, the number one is assigned to the sun. People whose lucky number it is, including anyone born under the sign of Taurus, will find the 1st and 10th of any month a fortunate time to begin new ventures.

TWO

Almost anyone with the lucky number two is likely to have a dual personality. They may also have psychic powers. The ancient Egyptians often carved lucky amulets in the shape of two fingers. They also frequently wore two feathers in their headgear, one signifying honesty and the other a symbol of knowledge. With two as your special number, your lucky days are likely to be the 2nd, 11th, or 20th of the month. Two is also a lucky number for persons born under the astrological signs of Cancer or Taurus.

THREE

Almost every religion has regarded three as a sacred and mystical number. It is also a lucky number for persons born under the signs of Cancer, Capricorn, Gemini, and Scorpio. The Egyptians worshiped the trinity of father, mother, and child. The Druids of ancient Britain considered three the number of their unknown, all-powerful god. Buddhists worship Buddha, his word, and his church as three in one. They also strive to attain three virtues: endurance, courage, and obedience. Christians regard God as the Trinity: Father, Son, and Holy Spirit.

The Romans wore rings engraved with three ravens to bring them luck in love. Gypsies, who also believe in the power of the number three, believe that if a dream comes three times, it will certainly come true.

If three is your own lucky number, your lucky days are the 3rd, 12th and 30th of the month.

FOUR

Four was considered sacred to Horus, the sun god of ancient Egypt, to Baal, the supreme god of the Babylonians, and to the sun itself. For all these reasons, it is regarded as one of the luckiest of lucky numbers. This is the only exception to the belief that odd numbers bring more luck than even ones. People with four as their number are likely to become powerful and successful. This includes those born under the signs of Aquarius, Gemini, and Virgo. Their lucky days are the 4th, 13th, 22nd, and 31st of the month. Sundays, no matter what the date, are also lucky.

FIVE

Often called the Soul Figure or the Figure of Life, five represents the center of all things. The five-pointed star is regarded by many as symbolic of geometrical perfection. Wizards and magicians in the Middle Ages wore them on their capes to symbolize the universe and all its mysteries.

The Bible tells us that Joseph presented five suits of clothes to his brethren and that he introduced only five of his brothers to Pharaoh. David took five smooth stones to overcome Goliath. Joshua hanged five kings from five trees. And most significant of all, every measurement in Solomon's Temple was either five or a multiple of it.

Muslims follow five articles of faith. Jews and Christians follow the ten commandments of God, a multiple of five. Among the Chinese, good fortune comes from five blessings: long life, luck, wealth, health, and peace.

Five is considered a lucky number for people born under the signs of Leo, Pisces, and Scorpio. Lucky days that go hand in hand with five are the 5th, 14th, and 23rd of the month.

SIX

The greatest students and thinkers have six as their lucky number. According to astrologers, Libra people influenced by this number will experience an event of great importance every sixth year. It is also lucky for those born under the sign of Aries. The influence is at its luckiest on the 6th, 15th, and 24th of the month.

SEVEN

Seven represents self-sacrifice and higher virtue. It appears repeatedly in Scripture in such things as the seven lamps of the temple, seven wise and seven foolish virgins, and Christ's feeding of the multitude with five loaves and two fishes. The early church taught that belief in God brings seven gifts: wisdom, understanding, honor, glory, blessing, strength, and godliness.

It is believed that the seventh son of a seventh son has the power of healing and that the seventh daughter of a seventh daughter has the gift of interpreting dreams.

Lucky days that complement seven are the 7th, 16th, and 25th of the month. Seven is lucky for people born under the signs of Aries and Capricorn.

EIGHT

Although it is not generally considered as lucky as other numbers, eight is believed to be favorable to people in the middle and later years. It sometimes has a negative effect on the young, but offers hope that luck will change for the better as the years go by. Anyone whose astrological sign is Aquarius or Capricorn will find luck in the number eight. Lucky days for people with eight as their number are the 8th, 17th, and 26th of the month.

NINE

Nine is the sum of three, considered among the most powerful of numbers, multiplied by itself. If it is multiplied by any number, the digits of the resulting number added together will always be either nine or another of its multiples. Because of these things, nine is considered a mystical number that has held an important place in most ancient traditions. Many of history's most powerful amulets contained nine stones.

If nine is your lucky number, you will be especially lucky on the 9th, 18th, or 27th of the month. It is the lucky number of Sagittarian, the only sign with just one lucky number, as well as those born under the signs of Leo, Libra, and Taurus.

Oak

In New York City's Grand Central railroad station, many of the doorways are lavishly decorated with representations of oak branches. The same design also appears quite frequently in the architecture of the Italian Renaissance. And oak leaf clusters are used to add importance to military medals. In every case, the significance comes from the ancient Romans, who thought of the oak as a symbol of strength and believed that oak branches, either real or representations of them, would bring them luck in the form of strength.

The oak branches at Grand Central conveyed a wish to cross-country train passengers that they would find the strength to cope with the long journey. The patrons of the Renaissance believed that the strength of the oak would serve them in their often difficult climb to the top of society.

The ancients of northern Europe believed that oaks attracted lightning, and although that in itself wasn't a good thing, it also meant to them that the tree absorbed the power of the gods. They, as well as the Druids in Britain, worshiped the oak—but usually from a respectful distance.

ONYX

The black stone frequently used in rosaries has long been regarded as having the power to inspire deep contemplation. But the onyx also has its downside. Some people believe onyx necklaces can cause nightmares and depression. Some even go so far as to say that wearing this stone will lead to frequent arguments and, if worn in a court of law, can result in a lost lawsuit.

OPAL

In the Far East, necklaces and charms with opal stones are believed to make the wearer a truthful person. The stone is also believed to convey the gift of foresight and prophecy, but only for people with pure hearts. If the power of the opal is used for selfish purposes, according to the Chinese, it will bring the worst kind of luck.

PARSLEY

Although parsley has the ability to eliminate bad breath, which makes it a lucky plant for the person who sits next to you on an airplane, it was considered sacred to the dead by the ancient Greeks and Romans. As such, parsley has unlucky connotations today.

It is considered unlucky, for instance, to transplant parsley because it is believed such an act will result in a death in the family, or at the very least, the devil will take control of the garden. It is quite unlucky to be given a sprig of parsley as a gift.

But in medieval Europe, it was commonly believed that anyone who happened to witness the so-called Wild Hunt, a nocturnal procession of dead huntsmen, horses and hounds, would be immediately transported to a foreign land. The only way to prevent the unwanted trip was to chew on a bit of parsley.

PEARL

In ancient Egypt, pearls were considered unlucky for married couples. But in our time the belief has been reversed, and wearing a pearl necklace on their wedding day is a special lucky charm for brides all over the world. In the shark-infested waters of the South Pacific, divers frequently wear pearls as protection. In ancient Rome, pearls ground into powder and dissolved in

wine was the cure of choice for madness. Today in China pow-
dered pearls dissolved in water settles an upset stomach. It is a
cure that has stood the test of time.

PERIWINKLE

The trailing evergreen plant, often called myrtle, is believed
to have the power to deflect bad luck. In ancient France it was
called *violette des sorciers* (violet of the sorcerers) not only
because its flowers resemble violets, but because of the plant's
perceived ability to ward off evil spirits. In France and most
other parts of Europe, periwinkle is hung over doorways and
windows to keep evil away and ensure good luck. Tradition dictates that the plant can only be cut on the first, ninth, eleventh
or thirteenth night after the appearance of the new moon. It
can only be cut by someone who is pure in heart. In Wales, on
the other hand, it is considered quite unlucky for anyone, pure
or otherwise, to pick the flowers or cut the tendrils of periwinkle
plants. But the Welsh consider it very good luck to have the
plant growing in one's dooryard.

PETRIFIED WOOD

Ancient trees that were submerged in water, dissolved, and
replaced by the minerals from the water, are today called
petrified wood. Petrified wood is another form of fossil since it
was once living and the fossil itself is simply the remaining
imprint of the dissolved tree. Petrified wood contributes to
increased longevity and aids in healing and protection.

Since petrified wood is very ancient and contains such an element of the past, it is often used to promote the individual's appreciation of life. It is also said to help individuals realize their own potential to evolve intellectually.

Because of its connection with water, petrified wood is often a charm to protect against drowning. Also, because of the peculiar hardness of petrified wood, it is thought to be particularly adept at giving protection to its bearer.

If you are in search of a way to become a more positive individual, try wearing or carrying an amulet of petrified wood since one of its main abilities is that of averting negativity.

PHOTOGRAPHY

Tradition dictates that photographers refuse to take pictures of a woman in her wedding gown before the conclusion of the ceremony. This was because they feared that anticipating the union might be an unfair testing of fate, such that the wedding might not actually occur. This particular superstition originated from the ancient idea that a picture or painting of any kind steals the soul of the subject.

PIG

Among the Chinese, gold charms in the shape of pigs are believed to have the power to bring good luck to any business venture. Pig charms also bring luck to the Irish. But in the Emerald Isle, folk wisdom says that the charm must have a part missing. Little pigs are popular souvenirs among visitors to

Ireland, but the figures will always be without an ear or a leg. Otherwise they don't qualify as a lucky charm.

QUARTZ

For thousands of years, the quartz crystal has been used in rituals meant to bring about a much-needed rainfall especially by Native Americans and Aboriginal Australians. This stone is said to have a strong connection with water, and is also connected with protection and healing. Quartz also symbolizes the spirit and intellectual powers unique to the human race.

Oriental peoples have long valued "phenomenal gems" that show mystical or powerful qualities, and they saw the cat's-eye quartz as one of the most outstanding. This stone was believed to bring especially good luck and fortunate consequences to its owner. While the cat's-eye quartz itself is considered the most potent in facilitating good fortune, other forms of the cat's-eye stone are also beneficial, such as the alexandrite cat's-eye, the star-ruby and the star-sapphire.

The stereotypical "crystal ball" during the Renaissance was originally made from beryl rather than a clear quartz crystal, but quartz crystals were occasionally placed on an ivory base and semi-coated with gold to assist the magician as he delved deeply into the psychic mind.

The rose quartz has receptive energies that encourage feelings of love. Rose quartz inspires tranquility, cheerfulness, and unfailing loyalty in long-term relationships. One other type of quartz that makes the wearer receptive to good luck is the smoky quartz that when worn, can help conquer depression and sadness and can also be used as a general mood-enhancer.

Some people believe that placing a quartz crystal in the light of a full moon enhances its luck-giving powers. Then, by wearing or carrying the crystal you can ensure fortune and luck, relieve headaches or other minor aches and pains, and balance the body's energies to prevent the onset of illness.

Rabbit's Foot

As lucky charms go, the rabbit's foot seems to be one of fairly recent vintage, which may explain why it is the charm of choice for the ring that holds the keys to the car. There is almost no evidence that any ancient people ever carried a rabbit's foot for luck.

Among our more recent ancestors, the majority of believers were likely to be farmers. The most prosperous of them had large families to help with the work. In the natural world around them, the largest families seemed to belong to the rabbits. That gave humans the idea that these were among the luckiest of creatures. As a symbol of plenty and prosperity, they had no equal.

Through the Middle Ages, people who worked the fields had a terror of spirits lurking beneath the ground. Yet their friend the rabbit not only defied the fates by living underground, but raised its huge broods of young there. Surely that was a sign of special powers over the forces of evil. Folks also noticed that the animal dug its burrow with its hind legs.

In order to share the rabbit's good fortune, farmers began to save the rabbit's hind foot before tossing one into the stew pot for a hearty meal of hasenpfeffer. They believed that the foot was where the animal's luck was concentrated.

Of the two hind feet, the right one is most often used as a lucky charm. A host of ancient superstitions claims that the right side of anything is preferable to the left. But if you carry a rabbit's foot, it will be most effective in a left-hand pocket.

RICE

One of the oldest wedding customs in the world is to shower the bride and groom with rice. It comes from ancient China, where rice was a symbol of fruitfulness. In the Middle Ages, Europeans substituted wheat for rice, but the meaning was the same. In our time, birdseed is often used because it is considered to be less wasteful. And for generations, confetti has been used to fill the air with color and happy thoughts. But the symbolism is the same as it always has been, an airborne wish for good luck and abundance.

RING

As an ancient symbol of eternity, any ring is a powerful lucky charm. The idea of engagement dates back to the Middle Ages, when a man's gift of a ring was an invitation to a woman to live with him for a few months while he decided if he wanted her for his wife. Wedding rings were the creation of the ancient Hebrews, who believed that a bridegroom had to present his wife with something of value. Placing the ring on her finger in the presence of witnesses made the marriage binding. In medieval Europe, a ring engraved with the names of the three wise men of the Christmas story supposedly had the power to cure cramps. Later, the same kind of cure was attributed to rings fashioned from coffin nails. Signet rings were worn by the ancient Egyptians to bring victory in battle or to help solve difficult problems.

According to the Koran, King Solomon had a ring that not only helped him subdue his enemies, but gave him the power to transport himself and his court from place to place upon a magic carpet. In ancient Rome, rings engraved with a five-pointed star were among the most popular means of acquiring good luck. In the Far East, rings in the form of two intertwined snakes are believed not only to assure a long and prosperous life, but to give the wearer the power to settle arguments.

ROBIN

When colonists from England first arrived in America, they found the robins much bigger than the ones they had known back home. Actually, it was a case of mistaken identity. What they found was the American thrush, a bird with similar markings, including a red breast. But they transferred their Old World beliefs to the New World bird and declared the bird to be lucky. As a sign of spring, the robin could hardly be considered anything but a symbol of good fortune. But other beliefs are connected with the bird. Finding a nest filled with blue robin's eggs is a guarantee of good luck, as long as it is left undisturbed. If the first robin you see in the spring flies upward, you'll have good luck all day long. If you make a wish when you see one, it will surely come true. And if robins build their nest near your house, you'll have good luck all summer. If you see a robin first thing in the morning, you'll have a visitor that day.

RUBY

In the ancient Far East, it was widely believed that rubies could drive away evil thoughts. These red stones can also keep you from losing your temper, help you prevail in an argument, and make you cheerful.

Salt

Of course you know it is bad luck to spill salt, and that if you do, you should immediately toss the spilled grains over your left shoulder. The tradition goes deep into antiquity. Even in prehistoric times, salt was considered the staff of life. Because the ancients noticed that salt doesn't change its basic properties when combined with other elements, they thought of it as a symbol of immortality. Over the centuries, various customs and beliefs regarding salt have emerged. In ancient Rome, a newborn baby was welcomed into the world by having a bit of salt placed in its mouth to bring it luck and long life. In the Middle Ages, the dead were buried with salt sprinkled over their hearts in the hope of an afterlife. The Romans and the Greeks before them always added salt to sacrificial food and tossed it into their sacrificial fires. They considered it an affront to the gods if any salt should touch the ground.

That explains our modern aversion to spilled salt, but it also provides a clue to a basic belief about all lucky charms: Any charm, amulet, or talisman intended to bring good luck will lose its power if it is allowed to touch the ground.

SAPPHIRE

In the ancient Middle East, this blue stone was believed to have supernatural powers. It was said to have been the center-piece of King Solomon's ring. In India, it has the power to bring health and wealth. Among its other powers in other parts of the world are the ability to repel spiders, to protect virgins, to turn away envy, and to attract the attention of the gods.

SCARAB

The most common lucky charm in ancient Egypt was a representation of a beetle called a scarab. Its image was usually engraved on rings, but the bug appeared on other forms of jewelry, too. It was also a common temple decoration. A five-foot-long scarab sculpture weighing more than two tons graces the collection of the British Museum. It may possibly be the biggest lucky charm ever created. In the thirteenth century B.C., the Pharoah Amenhotep II had hundreds of scarabs carved, and he recorded noteworthy events of his reign on their backs. The image was also commonly used as seals on important documents.

But first and foremost, the scarab was a lucky charm. Soldiers wore them into battle. As a gift between friends, a scarab symbolized a wish for good fortune and a long life.

The inspiration for this veneration is a dung-eating beetle common in Egypt, but also found in all parts of the Middle East. Wherever it is found, it has enjoyed the same significance among ancient peoples. What is so special about this little creature is its peculiar lifestyle.

The scarab beetle has a habit of collecting a mass of dung, laying a single egg in the center of it and then kneading it into a ball about two inches in diameter, much larger than itself. Once having done that, the scarab turns its head away from the ball and begins pushing it with its hind legs. It will often go great distances traveling backward to keep the ball rolling. Its goal is a quiet spot where the warmth of the sun will hatch the egg.

From the earliest times, this action was symbolic of the act of creation and immortality. The ball the beetle pushed represented the sun. The Egyptian god, Khepera, was said to push the sun around the sky each day, giving mankind vital heat and light. It was obviously powerful magic, and transferred to the scarab, was capable of bringing not just good luck, but long life as well. Scarabs were invariably placed over the hearts of the dead during the mummification process. It was considered necessary if the deceased were to have any hope of an afterlife.

SERPENT

Although many people recoil in horror at the sight of a snake, the serpent has been a powerful luck-bringer since the dawn of time. The ancients believed that snakes had unusually

long lives because of their ability to shed
and regrow their skins. They associated
serpents with old age and the wisdom
that maturity brought. As a lucky charm,
a serpent with its tail in its mouth, forming a circle, was a symbol of eternity and
helped ensure long life. The Egyptian
pharoahs wore crowns topped with a representation of a cobra as a means of securing wisdom. The image is repeated over and
over in Egyptian tombs as a symbol of eternity, in the hope
that the suggestion would lead to a long and happy afterlife.
The Romans placed likenesses of serpents over their doorways
as a charm against illness within the household.

SEWING

Seamstresses, tailors, and women who make clothes for
their families follow traditions of luck that date back to the
Middle Ages. It has long been believed that dropping a needle
accidentally is a sign of good luck, but that dropping a pair of
scissors will bring bad luck unless one is careful to step on them
before picking them up. It is also considered bad luck to leave
an open pair of scissors, which forms a cross, on a table.

Among beliefs associated with sewing, it is considered bad
luck to begin work on a garment on a Friday unless it can be
finished before sunset. Similarly, it is very bad luck to sew at all
on a Sunday.

Shell

Seashells have been used as sacred objects and bringers of luck for thousands of years. As one of the emblems of Buddha, shells are a powerful symbol in the Far East. Early seafarers noticed that when they placed a shell against their ear, they could hear a sound very much like pounding surf. They interpreted that as a sign that the shell was a link between those on the high seas and those left behind on land. In that way, shells became lucky charms that could ensure a safe return from a voyage.

Shrunken Head

After the dinosaur skeletons, the most popular exhibition at the American Museum of Natural History in New York is its collection of shrunken human heads. Although they no longer practice head-hunting, the Jivaro tribe of eastern Ecuador and northern Peru collected these trophies for generations. To them, these grizzly heads, reduced to the size of an orange, were amulets that brought them luck. Warriors went into battle wearing them suspended from cords around their necks in the belief that the spirit of the person they had killed to obtain the trophy would give them strength and good fortune.

Sigil

A mystic word written or engraved on a talisman is called a sigil. *Abracadabra* is one of these words. Another, common in the Middle Ages, is *Agla*, formed of the first letters of the Latin for "Thou art mighty forever, O Lord." At about the time Columbus set sail for America, his contemporaries used the sigil *Anizapta* as a preventer of drunkenness. Presumably, if you could pronounce the word, you were probably sober.

The names of the three kings of the Christmas story, Caspar, Melchior, and Balthazar, were frequently used as a sigil to help one find anything that was lost. The names were scratched into wax tablets which, if placed under one's pillow, would produce a dream showing where the object could be found. The luck extended beyond material things and the sigil was believed effective in finding long-lost friends.

SILVER

Many lucky charms and talismans are considered more effective if they are made of silver. In China, a father who has only one son assures his offspring's health and safety by collecting one hundred silver coins from a variety of friends and melting them down to make a charm in the form of a padlock.

The ancient Persians believed that silver shields and breastplates made their soldiers invulnerable. Although Alexander the Great conquered them in spite of their protective armor, he was so impressed with their abilities, he outfitted his own soldiers in the same way. His army went on to conquer nearly all of the known world.

SNEEZING

It is almost a reflex action among Americans to say "God bless you" when someone sneezes. The custom, perceived as a wish for luck, goes back to America's European roots. In most parts of Europe, there is an old belief that a sneeze can expel the soul from the body. Because of this, the blessing serves as a verbal charm to protect the sneezer from death. Another belief is that if someone sneezes three times without receiving a "bless you" from someone, the fairies could come and take him away.

Sometimes, however, the blessing isn't completely necessary. A corollary belief holds that if two people sneeze simultaneously, both will enjoy very good luck.

A solitary sneeze is considered a lucky omen in many parts of the world. The Maori people of New Zealand believe it is symbolic of the act of creation. According to their creation myth, the first human received the breath of life when the great god Tiki sneezed. In parts of Africa, sneezing is considered a sign that the body has been taken over by good spirits. And most Native American tribes believed that a sneeze was a sign that the brain was being cleared of evil.

This superstition may also have arisen from a serious disease that was attacking the early Romans (around A.D. 150) and the main symptom was sneezing. This disease was so serious that people often died as a result, and the Romans believed that the more often the individual was blessed, the lower the chances of death.

Also, "God bless you" was a frequently used form of well-wishing at the time. It was considered a wish for good health, which is the reason it was addressed to those who were sneezing. Since sneezing was a symptom of the bubonic plague in the Middle Ages in Europe, the custom of blessing people after they sneeze persisted and has been handed down until today. For the Hebrews, Greeks, Indians, and Chinese, breath was a tangible sign of the soul's existence, and any loss of breath, especially in a sneeze, was exceedingly bad luck.

SOLOMON'S SEAL

Solomon, who was King of Israel in the tenth century B.C., and the son of King David, is considered one of the wisest men who ever lived. He was also a kind of mystic, an expert exorciser of demons and devils. Among his legacies is Solomon's Seal, a talismanic device in the form of a six-pointed star made up of two opposing triangles. One of them, with its points upward, represents the sky, fire and masculinity. The other, with downward-facing points, represents earth, water and femininity. By synthesizing these opposites, the resulting star has the power to invoke divine protection for anyone who wears it. A version of this hexagram, known as the Star of David, is the symbol of the Hebrew religion and appears on the Israeli flag.

SPIDER

One of the most enduring tales in the history of Scotland is about King Robert Bruce, who was proclaimed an outlaw in 1306 and forced to go into hiding. When everything looked hopeless, he noticed a spider swinging back and forth, patiently spinning a web. It was the king's lucky day. Inspired by the lesson in patience, he decided that the only way to regain his throne was to persevere as the spider had. It took him seven years to regain his crown, but after he did, his country became independent of the British, who had controlled it for three centuries. It was all thanks to a patient spider.

For hundreds of generations, killing a spider has been considered unlucky. Many believe that if you walk through a spider web, you'll meet a friend. A spider web in your bedroom is a sign of good luck all day long. But if you should happen to see the spider itself, you may have bad luck. On the other hand, a spider is a very lucky omen if you see one in your house in the afternoon. It is especially lucky if the spider's head is turned toward you.

SPITTING

Boxers usually spit on their fists before delivering what they hope will be a final blow. Gamblers spit on their hands to guarantee luck. Merchants spit on the first coin they receive each day to encourage more to follow. Aboriginal people in the South Pacific spit whenever the name of a dead person is mentioned. The ancient Greeks made it a point to spit three times when they saw a madman.

The custom of spitting for luck, fortunately, isn't as common today as it once was. But, for centuries, it has been a means of warding off evil and encouraging the interaction of good spirits. It began as protection from the evil eye. Just as it was believed that harmful effects could come from the eyes, it was thought that the body received bad spirits through the mouth. To avoid them, people simply spit them out. In most cultures, spitting three times was most effective, as the number three has long been considered magical.

STAR

You can thank your lucky stars for the ancient belief that every person has been assigned a special star of destiny. Even today, many people believe we each have a star with our name on it. It shines at our birth and goes dark at the instant of our death. In the meantime, it guides us through life and brings us luck.

Any charm in the shape of a star is considered quite lucky. One commonly used is the pentacle, the five-pointed star, which the ancients believed had the power to trap the forces of evil, rendering them powerless.

STEPHEN, SAINT

Saint Stephen was the first Christian martyr. He was noted for his strong personality and fortitude, as well as his eloquence and generosity. Since he was also considered a great preacher, he was reported to the Sanehedrin, the judicial body of the church. He argued his case before the assembly, but it was concluded that he was a blasphemer and he was taken out of the city and stoned to death.

Since stoning was a sharply painful way to die, Saint Stephen is now invoked by headache sufferers seeking relief from their own pain. Other martyrs who died by similar methods or by being beheaded are also invoked against migraines, headaches, and other forms of sharp pain.

Talisman

The word *talisman* is often used interchangeably with amulet and charm, but talismans have a meaning all their own. Ordinarily they are a stone, a piece of parchment, a ring, a bracelet, or a necklace inscribed with words or figures believed to have special powers. What sets talismans apart from ordinary charms and amulets is that they are more than just protective devices. They are stroked or touched for luck and frequently placed, over doorways for instance, where their powers are needed most.

Among the most common of talismans is the Saint Christopher medal, which many believe offers protection to travelers. According to tradition, as he approached martyrdom, Christopher asked God to protect wherever his body lay from disease and other misfortune. Early Christians began placing pictures of him on buildings and doorways, and eventually on medals in the belief that to see Saint Christopher is to be safe from harm.

Almost any religious symbol—the Christian cross, the Jewish mezuzah, the ancient Egyptian ankh, and the tiki figures worn by Polynesians—is a talisman. So are the representations of animals and gods created in primitive societies.

But even an article of clothing, a coin, or something belonging to someone near and dear can have talismanic powers. Some of the most sincere believers in such things are sports stars. Baseball pitcher Vida Blue had one, too. Like many ballplayers, Blue thought his cap brought him luck and never went to the mound without that one special hat. Over the course of several seasons it became a mess of pine-tar smudges, sweat, and ground-in dirt. It was fine by him as long as it brought him luck, which it seemed to be doing. But league officials thought it conveyed a bad image and threatened to suspend Blue if he didn't get rid of that hat. The pitcher finally agreed to begin wearing a new cap, but not before staging a pregame ceremony of burning the old one. He won the game that day even without it, possibly because he had treated his talisman with respect.

TATTOO

The word *tattoo* became part of the English language in the late eighteenth century, when the explorer Captain James Cook discovered the Hawaiian Islands and recorded that the Polynesians there made gashes on their bodies which they called *tatou*.

But even if the British didn't have a word for it until then, they had a long history of people marking their bodies to ward off evil, to signify status, and to bring good luck. When the Romans crossed the English Channel in the first century, they were stopped dead in their tracks on the way to what is now Scotland by a fierce tribe of Celts who painted their bodies blue. The invaders called them Picts, from the Latin word that meant "painted ones." The practice didn't seem odd to the Romans. They had seen women in Egypt following a centuries-old custom of tattooing their faces. And they had seen painted people in every corner of the empire.

In just about every case, the practice grew from a belief that symbols painted on or cut into the flesh would ward off evil and ensure good luck. Just as earrings and nose rings were created as a means of protecting exposed openings in the body, a scar or painted talisman on the neck or nose represented a more permanent means of warding off evil spirits lurking in the air.

In some cultures, the meaning of the marks went even further. Many Hindus believe that it is impossible to enter heaven without a tattoo. The belief is related to a long-standing tradition among soldiers, who wore tattoos to aid in identifying their bodies if they fell in battle. Without proper identification, they may not have received a proper burial. And that, they believed, diminished their chances of entering heaven.

Sailors, perhaps the most tattooed group of all, were responsible for bringing the art into the Western world from the Far East. They took to the practice like ducks to water, ordering individualized tattoos that would identify them if they were washed ashore after drowning.

Obviously, neither soldiers nor sailors believe such a fate is in store for them personally. But by preparing for the possibility, their tattoos really serve as lucky charms.

Theatrical Luck

Actors live in a world of make-believe, but luck is very real to them. It helps them explain how they got the part or, if their luck is bad, why they didn't. It helps guarantee a good performance, a long run, a rapport with the audience. So many things bring luck (both good and bad) in the theater that it is a rare actor who doesn't consider luck far more important than talent.

Among the things actors believe is that a bad dress rehearsal guarantees a good opening night. Some are convinced that the final lines must not be spoken until the opening because the last line signifies perfection, which must be saved until the critics are present. If you've ever wondered why the curtain doesn't go up on time, it's because the performers believe it is lucky to start the show thirteen minutes late. If one of them trips on stage, it is not a disaster at all, but a sign of good luck.

Almost every performer has a lucky charm of some kind. On opening nights, actor Glenn Ford always made it a point to wear a necktie he bought with his first paycheck as a juvenile player. Film director John Ford wouldn't think of shouting "roll 'em!" unless he was wearing his lucky hat. Opera singer Luciano Pavarotti never feels secure onstage until he has found a bent nail in one of the sets. The Shakespearean actor John Barrymore would never walk onstage until he had first eaten an apple. Tallulah Bankhead began a tradition that if champagne is spilled on opening night, it must be daubed behind the ears. She drank a great deal of champagne after performances, considering it a lucky thing, as most actors do.

Bad luck is always waiting in the wings, but fortunately it's avoidable. One way is never to whistle in the dressing room. If someone does, the person nearest the door will be fired. This custom has a practical origin, apart from the fact that the whistling can be heard by the audience. In the early days of the theater, stagehands moved the rigging that controlled the sets in response to whistled signals. One set out of place almost always resulted in disaster.

Opening an umbrella anywhere indoors is generally considered bad luck, but it's worse in a theater. Mary Poppins notwithstanding, theater people shudder even when an unopened umbrella appears onstage.

Although they are quite decorative, you'll never see peacocks or their feathers onstage. That superstition began centuries ago, when it was believed that the pattern of the feathers in a peacock's tail was a representation of the evil eye.

The colors yellow and green are considered bad luck by many actors. Yellow roses mean that death will come to a friend, and a yellow dog in a production dooms a cast member to death. In spite of the long and successful run of *Annie* on Broadway, whose best-loved star was a yellow dog named Sandy, many stage people still cling to this belief. Cats are also bad luck if they appear onstage, but are very good luck backstage.

In spite of their fervent wishes for good luck, it is dangerous to say "good luck" to a performer. They prefer to hear "break a leg," a wish they hope will fool the fates. Though legs have been broken onstage, it happens rarely enough to keep the custom alive.

Anyone who has been forced to memorize parts of Shakespeare's *Macbeth* in high school may agree with theatrical professionals that it is a cursed play. In fact, when it is performed, the name is used only on the theater marquee. Everyone inside, from stagehands to actors, call it either "the play" or "the Scottish play." Bad luck seems to have dogged it since its premiere in 1606, when the actor playing Lady Macbeth became ill and Shakespeare himself was forced to appear as his

understudy (women didn't appear onstage in those days).
The play wasn't performed again for fifty years. Yes, even
Shakespeare could have a run of bad luck. Over the years,
hundreds of productions of the play seemed to have brought
dis-aster: theaters burning, cast members dying, even riots and
earthquakes. When Sir Laurence Olivier played Macbeth, his
voice failed him. Then, as if to add insult to injury, a sandbag fell
on him. When Orson Welles tried turning the play into a
movie, he went bankrupt. Is the play cursed? Almost anyone in
the theater will tell you it is. And that may be why, although
Macbeth is required reading in many high schools, students rarely
get a chance to experience it performed by professionals. On
the other hand, the superstition might be unreasonable. Possibly,
as Macbeth said, ". . . It is a tale told by an idiot, full of sound
and fury, signifying nothing." But try telling that to Sir Laurence
Olivier or Orson Welles.

THUMBS-UP

If approval means luck, the thumbs-up sign is a lucky signal.
To the ancient Roman gladiators, it meant they would live to
fight another day. To us it is still a message of hope.

The significance of the thumb as a symbol dates to prehistoric people, who noticed that babies are usually born clutching
their thumbs. This was interpreted as the first sign of life.

Tiki

The Polynesians of the South Pacific wear tikis around their necks to protect them from witches and other evil influences. Most often carved from jade but sometimes of wood, the charm is in the form of a little human-like creature. Its head is tilted as if listening intently for evil lurking in the air.

Toasting

In the good old days it wasn't at all uncommon to slip a bit of poison into someone's drink. As a means of avoiding sudden death, people began requesting that their host take a sip or two from their glass. Eventually, it became necessary only to touch each other's glasses together making a sound that would frighten away evil spirits. The touching was accompanied by a wish for health, which was another way of saying "I haven't poisoned you."

In the days when wine and ale were drunk almost as soon as they were made, sediment collected at the bottom of the glass. The problem was solved by dropping a piece of toasted bread into the glass to soak up the bitter bits. The result was a tastier drink if not a healthier one. And that's how the term "toasting" came about.

Tommyknocker

Among the men who work in coal mines, spirits called tommyknockers are believed to work nearby, usually bringing them luck by forewarning disasters and leading them to rich veins of coal. Although usually friendly, tommyknockers sometimes have a malevolent streak. They are believed to be the force behind many a cave-in, and survivors have claimed that they heard their laughter as the roof fell in.

Tommyknockers are regarded as industrious and often work through the night uncovering seams of coal. Miners going into the shafts in the morning make it a point to listen for their mysterious knockings, which will lead them to a relatively easy day's work. They are often heard, but rarely seen. Those who have reported seeing a tommyknocker describe a miniature man, less than a foot tall. It is believed that these spirits detest whistling and it is considered very bad luck to whistle in a coal mine, lest the tommyknockers will be offended. It is also considered good practice to leave behind some tidbits from the lunch pail for them, and at the end of the workday when the men gather at the local tavern, they always leave a space or two at the bar for their tommyknocker friends.

Topaz

During the Middle Ages, when the cure for the common cold was as elusive as it is today, some people believed the cure had been found in the form of the topaz. This gemstone was believed to have the ability to raise one's body heat and promote sweating which, even then, was known to bring relief from colds and fever.

In many cultures, from South America to East Asia, the topaz has long been worn as a talisman to prevent greed in the wearer. At the same time, it encourages success in business and attracts money. In many parts of the world, topaz is given as gifts between friends to ensure that the friendship will last forever.

Totems

Native Americans, particularly in the Pacific Northwest and Alaska, carved the figures of birds and animals on upright posts not only to venerate the spirits of these creatures, but to bring luck to their tribes. The same kind of symbolism exists in Central Africa and on the islands of the Pacific. The custom was also prevalent in the earliest civilizations of Egypt.

Triangle

In engineering, the triangle is considered the strongest and most indestructible form for structures of every description.

Even before mankind began to realize this, practitioners of ancient religions found mystical significance in the shape of a triangle and frequently fashioned charms and amulets in that shape. It was perceived as representing the cycle of life—birth, maturity and death—and as such it stood for the harmony of humans with their gods. It was considered a sacrilege to break its perfect shape.

The ancient Egyptians used this holy shape when they created the great pyramids, which many today regard all by themselves as symbols of good luck even though they are in reality monuments to the dead. The architects who designed them combined four triangles as a symbol of the coming together of the forces of earth and of heaven.

In France, on the other hand, the triangle has long been considered an unlucky shape. The French believe that the devil is likely to be lurking at a crossroads or a field with only three sides. In the Western Hemisphere, quite possibly the unluckiest territory known to man is the infamous Bermuda Triangle, where ships and planes have been known to mysteriously vanish with unsettling frequency.

TRISKAIDEKAPHOBIA

If ever there were a number that could make people reach for their lucky charms, it is thirteen. The Greeks gave us a fancy word for our aversion to the number: *triskaidekaphobia*, a combination of *tris*, meaning "three," *kai*, which means "and," *deca*, their word for "ten," and phobia, "fear." In other words, three-and-ten-fear.

An origin of this fear is the Last Supper, where Jesus Christ was betrayed by one of His twelve apostles. If Friday falls on the thirteenth of the month, that's considered unlucky because tradition says that Christ was crucified on a Friday.

Another explanation comes from an old Norse tale of a feast attended by thirteen gods and goddesses. Among them was Balder, the god of all things bright and beautiful, and Loki, the god of mischief. Loki goaded Balder's brother into throwing a dart of mistletoe at Balder, killing him instantly.

A more scientific theory holds that in prehistoric times, when the concept of numbers first emerged, twelve was as far as anyone could count. The number that followed it was mysterious and inspired fear. As mathematics developed, thirteen seemed to stand alone as a completely indivisible number. It didn't follow any of the rules that governed the numbers below it. Obviously it was a number to beware of.

After Christianity was established, Satanic cults instituted the Black Mass as a mockery of the Last Supper. Their secret covens purposely included twelve witches and a leader known as a warlock. Church leaders saw the symbolism in the number and began teaching that thirteen was unlucky. As with other two-digit numbers, the result of adding the two was one of the keys to its power. In the case of thirteen, adding one and three gives you four, which had been a very lucky number to early sun-worshipers. The holy fathers interpreted this as a heathen-ish sign and warned their followers that thirteen was anti-Christian.

In merry old England, anyone condemned to die at Tyburn, the site of London's public hangings, was obliged to tip the hangman thirteen pence—proof that the number thirteen can be very unlucky, indeed. But not everyone has held the view that thirteen is unlucky. The Aztecs built sacred platforms with thirteen steps and built fires on top that were kept burning for thirteen years at a time. The Maya before them worshiped thirteen gods, no more, no less, and believed that the number itself symbolized one collective deity. On the other side of the world, followers of Buddhism still pay homage to thirteen Buddhas. The ancient Hebrews gave the number sacred status, too. The Book of Exodus tells us that God revealed himself in thirteen merciful attributes. The orthodox Jewish prayer book stresses the thirteen principles of faith. And Jewish children become full members of the community at the Bar Mitzvah or Bat Mitzvah, always at the age of thirteen. Astrologers who created the twelve signs of the zodiac made it quite clear that the sun influenced all of them, giving us, in effect, thirteen signs.

Because people who believe in the power of numbers hold that odd ones tend to be the lucky ones, there is a strong case to be made that triskaidekaphobia is nonsense. Among those who tempted the fates to prove it was basketball star Wilt Chamberlain, who always wore the number thirteen, no matter what team he played with. On the other hand, he always wore a rubber band on his right wrist to bring luck.

Less cautious was movie mogul Nick Matsoukas, who founded the National Committee of Thirteen Against Superstition, Prejudice and Fear back in the mid-1940s. He established his committee on Friday the thirteenth with twelve of his associates. Together they made it a point to hold off any important decisions until Friday, considered by many to be an unlucky day. If they left town on business, Friday was the day to start the trip. And they met together for dinner, all thirteen of them, every time the thirteenth fell on Friday. None of them ever seemed to encounter any bad luck, although they did all they could to court it.

Matsoukas himself had become a successful executive at 20th Century Fox in spite of the fact that his name had thirteen letters in it. But that wasn't all. He was the thirteenth child in his family. He was born on June 13, and as a young man arrived as an immigrant in the United States on the thirteenth of February.

Another man who rose above the threat of triskaidekaphobia was composer Richard Wagner. He never missed an opportunity to point out that his name consisted of thirteen letters. He was also pleased to note that he had been born in 1813. He composed thirteen operas during his career and finished his masterpiece, *Tannheuser*, on March 13.

Others who scoff at triskaidekaphobes like to remind them that the United States has survived quite nicely for more than two centuries under a flag with thirteen stripes on it. And no one, no matter how superstitious, would ever refuse to carry a dollar bill. On the back of the dollar bill, the eagle holds thirteen arrows in one talon and an olive branch with thirteen leaves in the other. Above its head are thirteen stars and it bears a shield with thirteen stripes. On the left side, above the pyramids, is the motto, *Annuit Coeptis* (God Has Favored Our Undertakings), which has thirteen letters.

TURQUOISE

The Indians of the American Southwest put great store in the power of turquoise to bring them good luck. Their jewelry still works its magic for modern Americans.

In Islam, the stone engraved with passages from the Koran is a luck-bringer that protects anyone wearing it from all evil by drawing it into itself. Muslims also believe that if the stone changes color, it is a sign of a woman's unfaithfulness.

Throughout history, the turquoise has been a symbol of friendship, often powerful enough to make a friend of an enemy. It has also been viewed as a valuable talisman for people who ride horses. The stone, some say, makes a horse manageable and can prevent nasty falls.

Turtle

In the Far East, a talisman carved in the form of a turtle is believed to have power over all kinds of bad magic. The Chinese and Japanese also wear charms in the form of turtles to insure long life. In ancient times, the shape of a turtle's shell suggested the dome of the sky and the creature became a symbol of heavenly virtue.

Turtledove

If a pair of turtledoves nests near your house, no one in your family will be troubled by rheumatism. In medieval Europe it was believed that holding a live turtledove against a sufferer's chest could cure pneumonia.

Umbrella

One of mankind's commonest beliefs is that opening an umbrella inside a house will bring nothing but bad luck. In some countries, the fates are also tempted if an umbrella is laid on a table. Neither belief can be said to hold water.

The bad luck attributed to umbrellas may come from the concept of sympathetic magic, the idea that imitating a force can create an opposite reaction. According to that kind of reasoning, opening an umbrella indoors when the sun is shining will bring rain. On the other hand, that could be a lucky effect during a drought. Those with more superstitious leanings suggest that an open umbrella inside a house is an open affront to the household gods. They will be offended by the suggestion that their protection against the elements isn't good enough.

Anyone who has ever been caught in a sudden downpour and remembered to take an umbrella along would consider it quite the luckiest of charms. In India, where the umbrella may have been invented, it is considered lucky even on sunny days. It is venerated as one of the eight glorious emblems of Buddha. And it was a symbol of royal power even before Buddha.

VALENTINE, SAINT

Since medieval times, Saint Valentine has been identified as the patron saint of lovers. For centuries, those who were in love and those who sought love have invoked his assistance on their behalf. In modern times, February 14, Saint Valentine's day, has always been considered a lucky day for those who wish to kindle or rekindle love.

VISUALIZATION

You may be your own most powerful source of good luck. If you wish to attract love into your life, all you may need is a bit of creative visualization.

Find a place where you are likely to remain undisturbed. Close your eyes, relax and imagine yourself in a warm and loving relationship. The partner you see in this image may not have a face—that is for the fates to provide. But as you sit quietly, let the warmth and pleasure you experience from your visualization permeate your being. If you hold in your hands one of the stones best suited to attract love, your visualization will make the attraction even stronger.

Wedding Luck

Few events in human life have more customs and objects related to luck than weddings. It is entirely appropriate, considering that this step may require more luck than any other.

The list of taboos to discourage bad luck and charms to attract good luck is almost endless. Most that are followed in America have come to us from the various European cultures. Among them is the belief that it is unlucky to marry after sunset, or on the birthday of either the bride or groom. It is believed that Thursday is an especially lucky day to get married, and in many parts of Europe, it has long been considered unlucky to marry on a Saturday—a belief that obviously didn't take hold in America, where it is far and away the favorite day. In some places, getting married on Monday is thought to bring wealth to the union, and a Tuesday wedding guarantees good health not only to the husband and wife, but to their offspring as well. In Catholic countries, where Friday is traditionally a fast day, it is still considered unlucky to marry on a Friday. Similarly, because the celebration after a wedding often tends to last into the wee hours of the following morning, Thursday is also considered an unlucky day for weddings.

Our European ancestors believed that it was lucky for a bridegroom to wear a new suit to his wedding. The luck would not last, however, if he ever wore it again, and the wedding suit was traditionally saved to be used as his burial clothes. Those same bridegrooms also put three grains of salt in their right-hand jacket pocket, and three coins in the left-hand one to bring luck to the marriage. Bridegrooms also wear a white carnation as the symbol of purity in love, admiration, and adoration. And to bring luck to the bride, they presented her with the shoes she would wear as she walked down the aisle, and always put a lucky coin in one of them.

It was believed that a bride would have bad luck if she made her own wedding dress. And she was tempting fate if she tried the dress on before the actual day of the wedding. She will also have bad luck, it is believed by some, if she looks in a mirror during the final fitting. She would have good luck in her marriage if she paid for the gown before sunrise on her wedding day. White has been the preferred color for wedding gowns for centuries. All other colors are believed to bring bad luck, especially green, the unluckiest color of all, not only for a bride but for her mother and her attendants as well. As a symbol of love and good luck, a rose must be given to a bride on the day of her wedding.

If the seamstress pricks her finger with a pin as she is working on the wedding dress, the resulting bloodstain on the fabric should not be removed. It will bring luck and everlasting happiness to the bride who wears it.

On the night before the wedding, the couple will have good luck if the groom breaks a plate on his fiancée's doorstep. During the wedding banquet the following night, the bride can ensure that good luck by breaking plates herself. This goes back to a very old belief that the sound of breaking dishes can drive away evil spirits.

Before leaving her father's house for the last time as a single woman, a bride should always break an egg with her left foot. But she'd better be careful. She will have bad luck if she breaks a heel on her wedding day or steps on the train of her wedding gown. On the way to the church, the wedding party should never take a detour or a shortcut. Bad luck will also follow if anyone in the group should see a policeman, a doctor, a priest, a lawyer or a blind man on the way to the wedding. Conversely, good luck will come to the marriage if the wedding party should encounter a black cat, a chimney sweep or an elephant. All should be careful to enter and leave the church by the same door to ensure luck.

Part of the ceremony in Jewish weddings is the drinking of a glass of wine by the bride and groom. When it is empty, the groom breaks it under his foot to bring luck to the marriage. One interpretation of this custom, which has been followed for centuries, is that it symbolizes new life because the broken glass can never go back to what it was before.

WEDDING RING

It is considered unlucky to ever wear a wedding ring on any other than the "medical finger," the only finger that has direct contact with the heart (the third finger). Courtship was significantly different in the past than it is today in that once romantic love was a kind of mating ritual that prepared the couple for the change from a single existence to a shared one and all of the life alterations that go along with it. In this way, circular rings were a symbol of fidelity and a symbol of trust between the two people, as well as a gift of precious eternity from God.

During the Victorian age in England, the wedding ring had even more of a symbolic and ritualistic position. Young brides-maids at a wedding would take the wedding ring and press the wedding cake through it nine times. This ensured that the unmarried virgin would meet her future love and be married within the year.

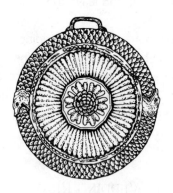

WHEEL

The flag of modern India has Buddha's Wheel of Life as its centerpiece. It was said that Buddha himself drew such a wheel in a rice field to teach his followers that all creation is a series of causes and effects following each other like the turning of a wheel.

As a circle representing eternity, the wheel appears frequently as a lucky charm in many cultures. It symbolizes that bad luck passes and good luck rises, just as a wheel is turned.

Lawyers in India nearly always wear wheel charms when they appear in court, and many believe they couldn't win their case without one. The ancient Romans usually depicted their goddess Fortuna with a wheel, symbolizing the same cause-and-effect relationship of bad luck turning to good that Buddha spoke of. It was this symbol that gave us the Wheel of Fortune.

Wishbone

In many households, after the holiday turkey has been picked clean and the bones set to boil for soup, one of them, the breastbone, is hung up to dry. When it becomes thoroughly brittle it will be a lucky charm called a wishbone.

The breastbone of any fowl will do, but one from a turkey or a goose is best because it is so large. Usually it is grasped by two people who close their eyes, make a wish, and pull it apart. The one with the larger portion can expect the wish to come true.

The wishbone is in the shape of a crescent and resembles a horseshoe, both powerful luck-bringers. It has been considered lucky for thousands of years. The Greeks and Romans, and the Chinese before them, relied on oracles to predict the future by studying the bones and entrails of birds. The breastbone was considered the most powerful predictor of all.

Even if they are not broken to make wishes come true, the wishbone's luck is proven at a venerable old tavern in New York City called McSorley's. For years its owner hung the wishbones from his Thanksgiving and Christmas turkeys over the bar. Over time he accumulated scores of them. They are still there, thick with dust, even though old John McSorley has been dead for a hundred years. Did they bring luck to the place? Established in 1854, today McSorley's is the oldest saloon in New York, a city where such establishments are lucky to stay in business more than a decade or two. In the 1920s, when selling beer and ale became illegal, McSorley's never closed. Was it the luck of the wishbones? Perhaps.

In England, these lucky bones are known as merrythoughts. In earlier times, it was believed that the person with the larger piece of a broken wishbone would be married first. The prospect presumably brought about pleasant thoughts, for which the Old English word was *merige*. Today, on both sides of the Atlantic, adding a gold or silver replica of a wishbone to a charm bracelet is a constant reminder that wishes can come true.

Yarrow

A plant with fern-like leaves and white flowers, native to Eurasia, but naturalized in western Europe and North America, yarrow was known to the ancients as the herb of Venus. Although its branches and flowers were believed to bring luck in love, the plant has other properties that make it valuable to grow. The ancient Greeks used it to promote nosebleeds, which they thought brought fast relief to migraine headaches. In Ireland, yarrow is a powerful protector against the wiles of one's enemies. An early Christian tradition holds that yarrow was the first herb touched by Jesus after his birth, which gives the plant the power to avert evil spells.

Yew

In Shakespeare's *Twelfth Night*, one of the characters exclaims, "Come away death ... my shroud of white, stuck all with yew." The Elizabethans considered the yew, one of the most common shrubs used in landscaping today, very bad luck. It was routinely planted in cemeteries, but avoided everywhere else. Sprigs cut from the shrubs were tossed into graves to keep the spirits of the dead in their place. And it was believed that to carry yew branches into a house was to court disaster.

ZIRCON

A zircon stone's powers are somewhat mysterious because it comes in many different colors and is known by several different names. But all versions contain important powers of magic and luck.

The main powers of the zircon include security, physical beauty, love and affection, tranquility, healing, and protection from theft. A yellow zircon is especially recommended to entice romance into the wearer's life, but it also reduces depression and aids in attaining business goals.

The red zircon commonly tends to increase the wealth of the wearer and protect him from injury.

If you are planning a vacation in the near future, try placing an orange zircon in your home and with any other valuables since its main power is to protect from theft. Similarly, carry an orange zircon with you on your trip and it may help protect you from injury and bring you safely home.

ZITA, SAINT

Zita was born in Italy in 1218 to a very strict Christian family. At age twelve she became a servant for a wealthy weaver, where she served until her death at age fifty. The other workers disliked her because of the efficiency with which she completed her tasks, and she substantially angered her master with her overwhelming charity to the poor.

Eventually, her good works won over her fellow workers and her master, and she was allowed to spend most of her later years pursuing charity and looking after the sick and poor. She was declared a saint by the people in Lucca, the town where she lived, when she died for all of her good and charitable works. The miracle attributed to her is that angels baked bread for her while she was praying. Since her domestic work was very much a part of her religious pursuits, she is the patron saint of maids, housewives, and servants, and the patron saint of lost keys.

BIBLIOGRAPHY

Ashley, Leonard R. N. *The Wonderful World of Superstition, Prophecy and Luck.* New York, NY: Dembner Books, 1984.

Batchelor, Julie Forsyth and DeLys, Claudia. *Superstitious? Here's Why.* New York, NY: Scholastic, 1954.

Bryan, J. III. *The Sword Over the Mantel.* New York, NY: McGraw-Hill, 1960.

Budge, E. A. Wallis. *Amulets and Superstitions.* New York, NY: Dover Books, 1978.

Burnham, Sophy. *A Book of Angels.* New York., NY: Ballantine books, 1990.

Caidin, Martin. *Ghosts of the Air. True Stories of Aerial Hauntings.* New York, NY: Bantam books, 1991.

Cohen, Daniel. *The Encyclopedia of the Strange.* New York, NY: Dodd, Mead, 1985.

Cunningham, Scott. *Cunningham's Encyclopedia of Crystal, Gem & Metal Magic.* St. Paul, MN: Llewellyn Publications, 1993.

Daniels, Cora Linn and Stevens, C. M. (Eds). *Encyclopedia of Superstitions, Folklore and the Occult Sciences of the World.* Detroit, MI: Gale Research, 1971.

Fewkes, Jesse Walter. *Hopi Kachinas.* New York, NY: Dover Publications, 1985.

Findlay, John M. *People of Chance.* New York, NY: Oxford University Press, 1986.

Fleming, Alice. *Something For Nothing.* New York, NY: Delacorte Press, 1978.

Frazer, Sir James G. *The Golden Bough.* New York, NY: The Macmillan Co., 1922/1958.

Funk & Wagnalls Standard Dictionary of Folklore, Mythology and Legend. San Francisco, CA: Harper & Row, 1972.

Guiley, Rosemary Ellen. *The Encyclopedia of Ghosts and Spirits.* New York, NY: Facts On File, 1992.

Guiley, Rosemary Ellen. *The Encyclopedia of Witches and Witchcraft.* New York, NY: Facts On File, 1989.

Gunther, Max. *The Luck Factor.* New York, NY: The Macmillan Co., 1977.

Hallam, Elizabeth (Ed). *Saints: Who They Are and How They Help You.* New York, NY: Simon & Shuster, 1994.

Huff, Darrell. *How to Take a Chance.* New York, NY: W. W. Norton, 1959.

Hultkrantz, Ake. *Native Religions of North America.* San Francisco, CA: Harper & Row, 1987.

Jones, Alison. *Saints.* New York, NY: W & R Chambers, 1992.

Kunz, George Frederick. *The Curious Lore of Precious Stones.* New York, NY: Dover Publications Inc., 1913.

Lasne, Sophi and Pascal, Adre (Eds). *Superstitions, from the Ridiculous to the Sublime.* Englewood Cliffs, NJ: Prentice-Hall, 1984.

Lockhart, J. G. *Curses, Lucks and Talismans.* Detroit, MI: Singing Trees Press, 1971.

Lys, Claudia de. *A Treasury of Superstitions.* New York, NY: The Philosophical Library, 1957.

Maloney, Clarence. *The Evil Eye.* New York, NY: Columbia University Press, 1976.

Marwick, Max (Ed). *Witchcraft and Sorcery.* New York, NY: Viking Penguin, 1982.

Morgan, Tom. *Saints: A Visual Almanac of the Virtuous, Pure, Praiseworthy, and Good*. San Francisco, CA: Chronicle Books, 1994.

Opie, Iona, and Tatem, Moira (Eds). *A Dictionary of Supersitions*. New York, NY: Oxford University Press, 1989.

Parrinder, Geoffrey. *Mysticism in the World's Religions*. New York, NY: Oxford University Press, 1976.

Perl, Lila. *Don't Sing Before Breakfast, Don't Sleep in the Moonlight*. Boston, MA: Houghton Mifflin, 1988.

Rachleff, Owen S. *The Secrets of Superstitions: How They Help, How They Hurt*. Garden City, NY: Doubleday, 1976.

Richards, Steve. *Luck, Chance & Coincidence*. San Bernadino, CA: Borgo Press, 1988.

Ruffins, Reynold and Sarnoff, Jane. *If You Were Really Superstitious*. New York, NY: Charles Scribner's Sons, 1980.

Sargent, Denny. *Global Ritualism: Myth and Magic Around the World*. Saint Paul, MN: Llewellyn Publications, 1994.

Stoddard, Lothrop. *Luck: Your Silent Partner*. New York, NY: Horace Liveright, 1929.

Sullivan, George. *Sports Superstitions*. New York, NY: Coward, McCann & Geoghegan, 1978.

Tallant, Robert. *Voodoo in New Orleans*. Gretna, LA: Pelican Publishing, 1983.

Thompson, C. J. S. *The Hand of Destiny: Folklore and Superstition for Everyday Life*. New York, NY: Bell, 1989.

Time-Life Library of Curious Facts: A World of Luck. Alexandria, VA: Time-Life Books, 1991.

Tuleja, Tad. *Curious Customs*. New York, NY: Harmony Books (Crown), 1987.

Tyler, Hamilton A. *Pueblo Gods and Myths*. Norman, OK: University of Oklahoma Press, 1964.

Tylor, Edward Burnett. *Religion in Primitive Culture*. New York, NY: Harper & Row, 1956.

Walker, Barbara G. (Ed). *The Woman's Dictionary of Symbols and Sacred Objects*. San Francisco, CA: Harper & Row, 1988.

Walker, Barbara G. *The Woman's Encyclopedia of Myths and Secrets*. San Francisco, CA: Harper & Row, 1983.

Weaver, Warren. *Lady Luck: The Theory of Probability*. Garden City, NY: Doubleday Anchor Books, 1963.

Wilson, Colin. *The Occult*. New York, NY: Vintage Books, 1973.

INDEX